Chris Brandon
Jan. 1973

Jan. 1973

D1206548

AUTOMOBILES & MODEL CARS
THE GOLDEN AGE OF MOTORING

With an introduction by Edoardo Massucci

CRESCENT BOOKS

Contents

All the photographs in this book were taken by Carlo Bevilacqua. The models themselves come from the collections of:
Alfa Romeo: 51
Carlo Brianza: 15, 32, 70, 89
Centro Storico Fiat: 14, 46, 63, 66, 92, 106, 109
Giuseppe Da Corte: 75, 84
Mario Grossi: 29, 35
Edoardo Massucci: 1–13, 16–23, 25–28, 30, 31, 34, 37–45, 47–50, 53–61, 64, 65, 67–69, 72, 76–82, 85–88, 91, 93, 94, 96, 100–103, 108, 111–114
Gianni Mazzocchi: 97
Mario Pestelli: 71
Roberto Tauschek: 73
The author wishes to thank the *Club delle Quattroruotine* for their co-operation in the preparation of the book

Translated from the Italian of Edoardo Massucci; English text supervised by Dr Cecil Gibson

© Istituto Geografico De Agostini, Novara 1971
Translation © Orbis Publishing Limited, London 1972
Printed in Italy by IGDA, Novara
Library of Congress Catalog Card No: 72-84381

Children play with toys and adults drive about in cars;
but except for those mundane souls who persist in regarding
the motor car simply as a means of transport, there may not
be all that much difference between the feelings
experienced by the young and the old. The car, in fact, is a
very large and splendid toy, and the fast-growing hobby of
model car collecting has renewed the interest of many
people in these fascinating objects, their erstwhile toy cars.

In this book, my old friend Edoardo Massucci has joined
a penetrating text to a collection of beautiful pictures,
and he has chosen to illustrate the history of the automobile
through the medium of models. Having seen his collection,
I know that he could equally well have illustrated the
stories of early Italian die-casts, tin-plate in the toy
industry, or the work of one of the master model makers
such as Conti. However, in this form his book has the
advantages of a historical perspective, and may also, I hope,
bring to the hobby some converts who had not previously
realized the pleasure of looking at today's beautiful toys.
He has, in fact, written the book that any fellow collector
and enthusiast would be proud to write.

Cecil Gibson

Models and scales

Everyone, whether interested in cars or not, old or young, has surely at some time stopped in front of a toyshop window and admired the almost incredible detail of midget cars. One can only wonder at such masterpieces of skill and patience, so accurately reproduced. During the last few years the art of making model cars – that is, exact miniature replicas of real ones – has progressed as rapidly as the development of the automobile itself.

The model car, or rather the toy car, has been with us for some time. In fact, the idea was first thought of at the same time as the car was invented. Old catalogues, dating back to the beginning of this century, and some even to the end of the last century, mention the first miniature cars, which were so highly priced that only the extremely rich could afford to buy them. However, apart from these few rare exceptions, true model car making only came into existence about forty years ago and was not really established until after the Second World War. In fact, it might be said that the art has only recently 'come of age' by turning away from the fantasy and play value of toys, towards greater realism and more faithful reproduction of the original. So we can now admire results that, a few years ago, were undreamed of. Such miniature masterpieces are now mass-produced and available to everyone, and there are also the remarkably beautiful hand-made models, which can be seen at exhibitions.

Before embarking on this history of the automobile, let us journey into the fascinating and picturesque Lilliputian world of its chief characters – the models. First of all the distinction must be made between industrially produced models, which can be bought in shops, and the hand-made ones, which are prototypes or unique models made by individuals, to whom this work may be a profession or merely a hobby.

The model car industry, which is well developed in the United States, Western Europe and Japan, consists of a large number of specialized factories. Some collectors' associations – which will be discussed later – have compiled a catalogue of all the model cars in the world, a kind of census of all the makes that once existed or still exist, and have gathered together the names of over four hundred model manufacturers. Of course, some of these firms are no longer in existence, and many makers cannot be considered truly specialized enterprises, and so after eliminating these companies, the present number of factories is estimated at around seventy. They are to be found scattered throughout the United States, Britain, Italy, France, Germany, Holland, Spain, Denmark and Japan.

Enthusiasts usually separate industrially produced models into two large categories: fully assembled models and assembly kits.

Fully assembled models may be made of metal or plastic, of varying types, dimensions and prices. At this point it would be as well to note that in speaking of model cars one often refers to the 'scale', which means the proportion between the dimensions of the real car and the model that is made of it. For instance, a 1:43 scale model has been reduced to one forty-third ($\frac{1}{43}$) of the size of the original. The scale of 1:43 was not chosen by chance. It is, in fact, the most common size in industrially produced models and is in greatest demand by collectors. Why 1:43 and not some other scale? The answer to this question lies with old model trains. During the 1930s miniature trains were made in O gauge, which roughly corresponds to the scale of 1:43, and model cars, which were at first merely accessories for these miniature railroad systems were naturally built to the same scale, so as to be in correct proportion to the trains. The success of these model cars, in particular the famous ones made by the American firm Tootsietoy, Meccano of Britain and Märklin of Germany, was beyond all expectations, surprising even the manufacturers themselves – so much so that they were no longer considered as mere railway accessories but as important objects in their own right. They were produced in vast numbers, and the demand has continued to increase up to the present day. The one thing remaining as a reminder of their former connection with toy trains is the 1:43 scale, which has been

4

The earliest commercial models were not always of particular vehicles. This is a 1904 clockwork model phaeton, made by Bassett-Lowke of Northampton, England, 'with Horn sounding Pip! Pip!'

retained in order to maintain continuity with the very first models. Furthermore, 1:43 scale has proved an ideal one from many points of view: for one thing it enables the maker to obtain a reasonable degree of detail – and hence realism – without posing a great problem of space to the collector.

With very few exceptions these 1:43 scale models were and still are made in die-cast metal, the material used being a zinc alloy known as zamak. Bars of zamak are placed in a furnace and melted at a temperature of about 2,300° Fahrenheit. The liquid zamak is then injected into the various moulds, where it cools quickly and solidifies into the correct shape. Finally, these moulded metal shapes enter a long assembly process which in large industries takes place on an assembly line. Obviously, the more complicated the model, the longer the assembly line.

The earliest zamak model cars of thirty or forty years ago consisted mainly of a shell for the body, a plate-like chassis to which were fixed two axles, and four tiny wheels made of metal discs shod with rubber. The rubber tire, which was a great achievement at that time, was to be one of the factors that brought such success to these miniatures.

Compared with the simple, childish models of those early days, the ones that are available today are real gems of perfection. The early models, such as the first Dinky Toys and Märklins, were made out of about ten separate pieces, whereas today they have fifty or sixty metal or plastic components. In order to satisfy the ever-increasing demands of the public, the manufacturers have incorporated more and more highly sophisticated and spectacular details into their work. It is now possible to find model cars with doors, trunk and hood that can be opened, seats with adjustable backs, tops that can be folded back, suspensions, operable steering, an exact reproduction of the engine, all inside fittings, lights and indicators that work, wheels that can be taken off and a host of other minute gadgets that make them more and more like real cars. A huge variety of types and makes is available: racing and record-breaking cars; veteran and modern cars; sports cars and austere official limousines. The model car industry follows the real motor industry step by step, always keeping

up to date. Today, there must be few vehicles of any importance that have not been reproduced in a scale model, and, in some cases, the motor manufacturers even collaborate with model car factories, so that a miniature car can come out at the same time as the real one is launched on the market. This has happened in several countries.

A good deal has been written about 1:43 scale models because, as mentioned previously, they are the most common and most preferred by collectors. This will obviously be reflected in the illustrations following this text. However, it should not be forgotten that excellent models can be bought in a number of scales. The scale varies from 1:10 in the largest models to 1:86 for the micro-models. A collector who does not want to observe rigid uniformity of scale or who prefers a scale other than the standard 1:43, can easily find a varied and interesting series of models. The older large-size models made by the Turin firm of Pocher, the modern 1:16 Fiats made by the same firm, the 1:25 die-cast models made by Politoys and Togi, the Schuco Formula racing cars and the micro-midgets made by Matchbox-Lesney are just some examples of such models.

Assembly-kit cars

So far only the ready-made models have been dealt with. The other type of mass-produced model, the assembly kit, came into existence at the beginning of the 1950s. In the USA, these kits, which were made up of several pieces, were greeted with an enormous enthusiasm that continued for about ten years. The assembly kit provided a new and amusing hobby, that of piecing together and personalizing many different sorts of model automobile, using parts supplied in kit form.

Although some of them were made of wood or metal, the huge success of these kits was due mainly to the fact that most of them were made of plastic. The craze soon crossed the Atlantic, and European shops were filled with American models by Revell, Monogram, Pyro, AMT, ITC and

5

By 1912, more and more model cars appeared in mail order catalogues. This one, which 'will run forward, backward or in a circle and can be stopped', was marketed by Sears, Roebuck & Co.

Aurora, to name but a few. Some Europeans attempted to follow the American example, but competition from the huge American firms was too great. Probably the only European firm that really succeeded in catching the market was the British Airfix Company, which, after its pioneering days, was able to maintain high sales with continuous and high-grade production.

After more than ten years of American monopoly, the Japanese took over the construction kit business and flooded the foreign market with assembly kits of every type and price. The only difficulty facing the collector and the enthusiast is that of choosing from the vast number of kits available.

A kit can consist of thirty to several hundred pieces, and there have even been some rare cases where the number reached 1,800. The beginner would be well advised to start with simple, low-cost kits to get his hand in without risking disaster. For the sake of those who have not seen an assembly kit, most of the components are arranged on a plastic framework, somewhat like fruit hanging from a tree. The car is assembled by detaching the pieces from the framework, and sticking them together. There are often also some larger pieces that are not attached to this framework, and lie separately in the box. The plastic parts are stuck together with a special cement, tubes of which are usually included in the kit. After the cement has dried, the model is painted with a special enamel paint, which is applied with a small brush and dries very quickly. On no account should cellulose or paint intended for metal be used, because they dissolve the plastic. In addition, no cement should be allowed to come into contact with the painted parts.

Once the art of assembling a kit has been mastered, the advantages over the factory-assembled models soon becomes obvious. Any number of modifications and elaborate details can be added to these models, and with a little patience and skill some real miniature masterpieces can be achieved, which may prove the starting point for more ambitious projects such as building models with hand-made components.

Fine craftsmanship

The art of building totally hand-made models has attracted innumerable followers all over the world. Some of these craftsmen are simply amateurs but a number are highly trained specialists who have dedicated their lives to this profession. Don Oreck of America, Wingrove of England, Conti of Italy and Olive Sans of Spain are only some of the many respected names in this field.

The models which these wizards of the miniature produce, can be of such perfection that even the most experienced person looking at a photograph of one of them is quite unable to say whether it is the miniature or the real thing. Amateurs and professionals may sometimes spend up to two or three thousand hours working on one of these amazingly realistic cars, so it is hardly surprising to learn that such masterpieces fetch astronomic prices, occasionally as high as for a full-size car. Even though the engines of such models are reproduced in every detail, only rarely do they function. The models are simply objects to be put in a glass case and admired. One good reason for not making working motors is that the model could easily be damaged in the process, and anyway it is almost impossible to make a fully operational engine with four, six or eight cylinders on such a small scale. Nevertheless, all the accessories and mechanical parts can be made to work, even though they are so small. The detail that can be achieved is almost unbelievable: models have been made with independent suspension on all four wheels; steering that really works; doors, hood and trunk that can be opened; winding windows, locking doors, and an electric light circuit operating the headlights, indicators, sidelights and brake-lights. Then there are windshield wipers, horn, and brakes operable by the brake pedal. Even the minute door handles can sometimes be turned. The seats and the whole interior of the models are padded and lined, there are spoked wheels, microscopic badges, tops that fold back, number plates and dashboards with all the correct instruments.

In constructing the bodywork, these craftsmen carefully

6

follow the same procedures used by old coachbuilders in beating out the body, rubbing down and preparing the surface, and painting. Some have even obtained excellent results with fibreglass bodies. To the uninitiated, it may be surprising that the most difficult task in this type of model building is neither construction of the bodywork nor that of the host of other mechanical parts just described, but making the tires. However, although this aspect does present the greatest problems, the more expert craftsmen have overcome this, either by designing very costly moulds for the rubber, or by cutting the tread by hand in a bakelite-type material.

Both factory and hand-made models have gained considerable popularity over the last few years. This popularity has led to the formation of clubs, the publication of specialized magazines and the setting up of exhibitions in a great many countries. And to make this brief survey of the world of model making complete, we should mention some of the many initiatives which have done much to further interest in this subject.

About fifteen years ago in France, a group of model makers and collectors of miniature cars formed a club which they called CIAM. It was the first association to publish a catalogue of model cars, while at the same time organizing the first exhibitions in Paris. Similar associations were founded in the United States and here the first publications on model cars were launched. In Italy too, new ground was broken. In 1960 the magazine *Quattroruote* ('four wheels') promoted the setting up in Milan of the *Club delle Quattroruotine* ('four tiny wheels'), whose aim was, as laid down in its rules, to 'unite, assist and advise those automobile lovers who collect miniature reproductions of motor vehicles'. Periodicals specializing in model automobiles are also published in a great many other countries.

Collecting model cars is a modern, amusing and instructive hobby because it enables the collector not only to become familiar with the world of automobiles but also to understand its historical background. Contrary to what is sometimes believed, this is not just a pastime for the very young; there are also a great many professional people – both male and female – fathers with grown-up children, and elderly people, who take pleasure in building, assembling and collecting miniature cars. In a great many countries there are opportunities to admire fabulous private collections consisting of five or six thousand models of every kind, including many very rare pieces. These rarities are usually antique toys – quaint little tin cars of the last century – which were made in limited numbers or by firms which have long ceased to exist. The ultimate goal of the true collector is the search for and the joy in discovering these rare items. And in the same way, the finding of a complete novelty is an exciting way of bringing a collection up to date.

Collections of five or six thousand models have been mentioned, but these are obviously extremely rare cases. The average collector can get enormous satisfaction from collecting and organizing just a few examples. For instance, it is fun to have a specialized collection of just one type or make of car, one particular period or size, or even a collection of all the work of one model maker. A very interesting possibility, which can be most spectacular as well as instructive, is to build up a collection that is arranged historically. In this way each of the various stages in the history of the automobile is shown, from the time of the early pioneers to the birth of the modern automobile. In fact, the aim of this book is to do just this.

The automobile's history

'A means of transport for use on roads, having four wheels and propelled by its own power' – this is how the most authoritative dictionaries define the word 'automobile'. Today, most people automatically think of an automobile as being driven by an internal combustion engine, but the history of the automobile goes back further than that of the combustion engine. Steam and electric motors preceded those driven by gasoline, and played vital roles in the early development of the automobile. In 1769, during the reign of Louis XV of France, a curious and rudimentary

7

A touring car from the same Sears Roebuck catalogue of 1912, this one rather less expensive than the model in the previous picture. Its tires are of metal, painted to imitate rubber. The toy cost 98c.

three-wheeled wagon, driven by steam, succeeded in puffing forwards for a few dozen yards under its own power. It was designed by an army engineer, Nicolas Joseph Cugnot, who had been instructed to build a tractor for heavy artillery, and put into practice what he had learned while building steam machines. This experiment was such a daring and memorable one that today automobile historians are unanimous in quoting it as the first example of mechanical locomotion. It is therefore logical that a model of this steam vehicle should start the illustrated history of the automobile; the one chosen is a French assembly kit model known as 'Precisia'.

For over a century the steam vehicle's only rival was the horse-drawn carriage, yet the steam vehicle was always an object of great curiosity and frequently of extreme hostility. People who were prejudiced against it went as far as to consider it the devil's invention. The first railroad companies were in agreement with the public in its distaste for the steam vehicles. In England, the railroad companies made applications to have special laws passed to limit development of these new vehicles, and in 1861 the Locomotives Acts were approved. Despite these measures, picturesque horseless carriages and gargantuan steam diligences could be seen trundling triumphantly around the dusty eighteenth-century streets, causing amazement and curiosity everywhere. Original engravings and surviving replicas give a clear picture of those old days, and also reveal other ancestors of the modern automobile. The most noteworthy of these include the Trevithick steam carriage of 1803, Griffith's steam diligence (1821) and also the diligences made by Goldsworthy (1825) and Hancock (1829), the hackneys made by Church, Hill and Macerroni in 1830, the street train made by Dietz in 1832 and the steam landau made by Bordino in 1854. The United States was not far behind in the development of a steam vehicle; the first three cylinder dates back to 1788. Here again this revolutionary means of transport quickly found admirers.

It is important to note that during these early days of the steam vehicle, the aim was not to create a means of private transport, but rather of public transport, like the diligences.

At the end of the last century, as Daimler and Benz began work on the internal combustion engine, the steam engine continued to have fervent admirers. And, before it was finally abandoned because of its limited range and impracticality, it had a reasonably long life. Among these dinosaur-like machines, a certain amount of fame was achieved by Scotte's steam vehicle in 1892, the 'Obéissante' ('the obedient one') made by Amédée Bollée in 1872, which owes its name to its great manoeuvrability, and the 'Mancelle' also made by Bollée in 1878, which was to earn the admiration of the Emperor François Joseph.

One of the first speed records was made in 1902 by a steam vehicle driven by the French engineer, Léon Serpollet. He had designed a machine with a flash boiler in 1888, and fourteen years later he completed another which he drove to Nice, breaking the world speed record by reaching a speed of 75 mph. Another memorable victory, this time when the era of the combustion engine had begun, took place in 1894, when a steam car made by the French firm De Dion & Bouton won the Paris-Rouen race – the first automobile race in the world.

Electric cars also found some success at the turn of the century. The storage battery, invented by Gaston Planté, and the various improved versions made by other engineers, made it possible to build automobiles with electric motors. But as with steam earlier, this method of locomotion had many limitations, owing to the great weight of the accumulators and the limited distances over which the cars could travel. But in spite of this, electric cars did have their day and left their mark on the history of the automobile. It was a single-seater car driven by an electric motor which became the first to reach a speed of 60 mph. This record was set in 1899 by the Belgian driver and car builder, Camille Jenatzy, in a curious torpedo-shaped car which had been given the strange name: 'Jamais Contente' ('never happy').

However, despite these encouraging results, it was the internal combustion engine that was to determine all future steps in the development of the automobile by enabling it to achieve possibilities that had previously been undreamed of. This field also had many pioneers whose experiments

8

and hard work contributed greatly to this brilliant invention, and hence to the history of the motor car.

Engineers and engines

The idea of using the force of an explosion and transforming it into a driving force had occupied the minds of several scientists, but though in theory this was a perfectly valid principle, the real difficulty lay in controlling the force of the explosion. (A very similar problem occurred not so many years ago, but on a far larger scale, regarding atomic energy.) The main problem was to find a suitable combustible fuel, and before gasoline was discovered, coal gas and other explosive fuels were tried.

In 1807 a Swiss called De Rivaz patented a motor driven by combustible gas and fitted it to a carriage. This was a significant event, but over three decades passed before two more inventions furthered the progress of the combustion engine. The first of these, in 1841, was the 'igneous-pneumatic' by the Italian, Luigi De Cristoforis, a machine which ran on a mixture of air and liquid fuel. Thirteen years later, in 1854, two physicists from Tuscany, Eugenio Barsanti and Felice Matteucci, patented a three-stroke combustion engine, and by two years later it was operational. Of course, both of these were initially fixed engines, but they soon progressed from the experimental stage to a practical achievement, and were thus very promising developments.

By this time, almost all the experts were convinced that the future lay in the internal combustion engine, and so in Europe and elsewhere they began to work feverishly, each one hoping to be the first to perfect the machine that would motorize their nation. In the years to follow, the history of the automobile quickly gathered momentum.

The Germans Karl Benz and Gottlieb Daimler, each working independently, succeeded between 1885 and 1886 in patenting their inventions, rudimentary but light and functional engines. Thus the combustion engine was born, and with it the modern automobile. What did these first automobiles look like? Daimler, as other technicians of the time, dealt with the problem of mounting the engine very simply: he took an ordinary horse carriage – known as a 'break' in those days – and with a few modifications adapted it to carry his vertical-cylinder 462 cc engine which was cooled by water. Karl Benz, however, decided that his engine would be better housed if he built a special three-wheeled car for it, and in fact it did give a more satisfactory performance. It had a single-cylinder 980 cc engine and was an enormous success at the Paris Fair of 1887.

Both Daimler and Benz soon had interesting offers from people who wished to buy their patents for commercial purposes and so the French companies Panhard & Levassor and Peugeot began to build cars as Daimler agents, while Emile Roger made a contract with Benz and became his representative in France. Between 1890 and 1900 the big automobile adventure began and the frenzy spread to all the principal countries in the world. At first France led the field, and in 1891 Panhard & Levassor, who had bought the Daimler patent, fitted their internal combustion engine to one of his cars. This vehicle travelled through the streets of Paris, covering a distance of six miles without any breakdowns – a real triumph! Other French companies were quick to follow their example, and the motoring world soon became familiar with names of the brothers Peugeot and Renault, Albert De Dion and Georges Bouton, Gobron and Brillié, Delahaye, Mors and Darracq.

Meanwhile in Germany, as his patents brought huge success to the French motor companies, Karl Benz continued experimenting, and in 1893 he brought out his famous 'Victoria'. This four-wheeled vehicle had a rear-mounted single-cylinder 2123 cc engine, and was a great improvement on the previous tri-car.

Italy too, which had obtained good results with fixed engines, was now able to move forward into automobile construction thanks to the ingenuity of Professor Enrico Bernardi. In 1883 this distinguished scientist from Verona built two combustion engines which he called Pia and Lauro. Then in 1894 he designed and built a little three-wheeled vehicle which was the first Italian automobile to be driven by a gasoline engine. This potentially great

9

The third and final example from the 1912 Sears Roebuck catalogue is also not of a specific model, but is described simply as a 'white enamel toy automobile'. With rubber tires, it was a bargain at 69c.

invention could have led to the formation of a large industrial enterprise. But the greatness of Professor Bernardi and his invention were ignored by those who might have helped him, and his work remained merely another significant episode in the history of the automobile.

In the sphere of racing, however, Italy was well to the fore. The race from Turin to Asti and back, covering a distance of 70 miles, was the first to be held in Italy and the second in the world. Five cars took part in it and the winner was a Daimler Omnibus, the only vehicle to reach the finishing post.

The first Ford car

In the United States, which was to become the home of the largest automobile industries in the world, the new motor carriages were at first given only a very tepid welcome and thought something of an enigma. But there was certainly no lack of pioneers. Among these were two brothers, Charles and Francis Duryea, who between 1882 and 1895 designed and built a light vehicle with a gasoline engine which has gone down in history as being the first American automobile. This Duryea also set another record: it beat all the other cars in America's first automobile race, which took place in 1895 from Chicago to Evanston and back, covering a distance of 50 miles – at that time almost a marathon!

As we have said, the automobile met with some resistance in its early days in America, and before it became regarded as a necessity the car builders had to work very much in the background. Gradually, however, towards the end of the nineteenth century, some people, who are now household names, began to attract attention. Studebaker, for example, who had been known as a carriage builder since 1849, began constructing electric and gasoline vehicles. In the spring of 1896, in the town of Lansing, Ransom Eli Olds, founder of that colossal industry that would produce the Oldsmobile, made his first run in a 'horseless carriage' he had built himself.

Packard, Rambler, Buick, Cadillac, Lincoln and

Chevrolet – to name only those whose businesses have survived to the present day – were other automobile makers who at that time were only formulating their ideas, but whose names are to appear again and again in this history of the automobile. In Detroit a man who had just emigrated to America, decided to try his hand at making machines. His name was Henry Ford and a few years later his ingenious ideas were to revolutionize the automobile industry and provide the decisive move towards the modern car. In fact he started the automobile industry proper and provided the decisive move towards the modern car. His first automobile, a curious four-wheeled cycle driven by a two-cylinder, 5 horsepower engine, came out in 1896.

By the end of the nineteenth century, the automobile industry in France was well on its way to great popularity, whereas in England its development was restrained by the rather bizarre laws which were incorporated in the Locomotives Act.

These restrictive measures came into being between 1861 and 1865, and were enough to discourage even the greatest enthusiasts. For example, Article Two reads as follows: 'A mechanical vehicle may only be driven on the highway when preceded at a distance of 50 yards by a man on foot holding a red flag'. Another law limited vehicles to a maximum speed of 10 mph on all roads; fortunately, however, these laws were revoked in 1896 and the British quickly made up for lost time. The same year also saw the opening of the first English Daimler factory, and three years later London had its first Motor Show.

Meanwhile, in Italy, the opportunities of which Professor Bernardi had failed to take full advantage were soon taken up by a native of Turin, Giovanni Battista Ceirano, who was making bicycles under licence from a British company. In 1898 he opened the first automobile factory, which adopted the name of this British firm, Welleyes. Shortly afterwards the inventor and engineer Aristide Faccioli founded Ceirano & Co., a small company with an equally small capital, which aimed to build prototypes of the new motor vehicles.

In 1899, on the initiative of a group of men who had in

10

common a passion for cars and a desire to establish a totally new industry, the company FIAT (Fabbrica Italiana Automobili Torino) was born. This factory, which was later to become one of the largest industrial complexes in the world, opened its first workshop in Corso Dante in Turin, and proceeded with its work so fast that by the end of the same year the first Fiat car was released on the market. This was the famous $3\frac{1}{2}$ hp model that has become the symbol of the company. The car was designed by Faccioli (Fiat had by now taken over Ceirano & Co.) and had a rear-mounted engine with two horizontal 679 cc cylinders. Encouraged by this first achievement, they brought out the 6 hp, which was similar to the $3\frac{1}{2}$ hp but with an engine capacity that had been increased to 1100 cc, so that it was capable of a speed of 25 mph.

The 8 hp model, which was made between 1901 and 1902, had a front-mounted engine and was one of the last vehicles to have a coiled radiator. In fact the coiled radiator was a constant source of disagreement between Agnelli and Faccioli, who left Fiat in 1901. Later, when the 12 hp model was built, it was fitted with a honeycomb radiator. By now the Turin company had got well under way and was shortly to take part in big motor races, which will be discussed shortly.

In 1899 Isotta Fraschini which was to bring such prestige to the Italian motor industry, was brought into being, and in the same year Bianchi produced its first car. Then, in 1904, the Itala arrived, in 1905 the OM-Zust, and in 1906 the Lancia was created by Vincenzo Lancia who had been a Fiat racing driver.

Unfortunately, it is quite impossible in this small space to mention all the significant events of the early years of this century which contributed to the development of the automobile. Everywhere there was a growth of initiative, and continual competition to find the best possible solutions to problems of design and construction. This involved men from every walk of life who by now had no doubts as to the uses of this new machine and the brilliant future it would have; few could have anticipated its importance in the later part of the century.

Race tracks and rallies

As the automobile industry grew and expanded, an enormous enthusiasm for motor sports developed, and in every country motor races, big and small, became common events. It was not just a passion for speed that impelled these racing pioneers to risk their necks on dangerous roads, at the wheel of noisy, unreliable vehicles. Engineers, technicians and drivers were all equally convinced that the best way of testing an engine, mechanical parts and accessories was on the race track. In addition, these races were useful for reasons of prestige, for to win one of these competitions brought the makers fame and ultimately commercial success. So they were the most immediate and effective forms of publicity. The first competitions were run on the open road, with all the contingent risks both to the competitors and to the occasional spectators; only later did the organizers change to special closed tracks for reasons of safety.

One of the most significant of the early races was the Paris–Bordeaux run of 1895, not because of the fame of the competitors but because this was the first time that the Michelin brothers fitted detachable rubber tires to a Peugeot.

In the early years of the century, long-distance races were very much in vogue. Among these were the famous Paris–Berlin run of 1901 which was won by Fournier at an extraordinarily high average speed of 45 mph, the exhausting Paris–Vienna run in 1902 in which Marcel Renault completed the course in 15 hours 47 minutes, and finally the tragic Paris–Madrid of 1903 which had to be abandoned because of the horrifying number of accidents involving spectators and competitors. One of the most famous competitive events was the celebrated Gordon Bennett Cup, inaugurated in 1900, which was run annually on various courses in Europe until 1905. Its rules stipulated that the competing cars had to be built entirely in the country of their origin. The Cup was instituted by an American businessman, James Gordon Bennett, son of the proprietor of the *New York Herald.* This popular race, organized by the French Automobile Club, drew some of the best racing drivers of these times such as Jenatzy, Thery, Cagno and Nazzaro. A similar trophy, the Vanderbilt Cup, was instituted in 1904; its rules were almost the same as those of the Bennett Cup, but it had to be run on the Long Island track.

The Gordon Bennett Cup was succeeded by the French Automobile Club Grand Prix which was often an extremely exciting race, as for example in 1907 at Dieppe, when the famous Fiat F2 driven by Nazzaro won the trophy. The Emperor's Cup was held in Germany at Taunus, and in Italy the Targa Florio was inaugurated in 1906 with victory going to an Itala driven by Cagno.

This was also the time of the great long-distance races – the 'marathons' – which were sometimes over entire continents with individuals or groups competing. When one considers that these great endurance tests were run on almost impassable roads, deserted areas sometimes way off the beaten track, without any aid, quite cut off from the rest of the world, one cannot help but call them truly legendary events. In April of 1902 an immense Panhard & Levassor berline which was named 'Passe Partout' left France for a round-the-world trip, the two drivers planning to go first to Russia, then China and from there to Vladivostok, then on to Japan and America. Unfortunately, after many adventures, the courageous pair failed when they reached the icy Russian steppes. Another memorable journey which had more success was the one undertaken by Charles Glidden between the years 1902 and 1907, when he travelled 50,000 miles across 35 countries in a British car, a Napier, without any problem at all. In 1903 a small-size Packard called the 'Old Pacific', driven by the American Tom Fetch, successfully crossed the United States from San Francisco to New York in 61 days. A few years later in 1905 an equally adventurous Coventry to Constantinople run was made by the British driver Jefferson in a Rover.

Of all these exciting events, certainly the most famous was the 'Peking to Paris' – the marathon of marathons – backed by the French newspaper *Le Matin*, which challenged motorists to drive the 10,000 miles over uncharted regions. Several daring men took part in this exhausting competition and it was won by an Italian car and team, the 35/45 hp Itala driven by Prince Scipione Borghese. With him were Ettore Guizzardi, the mechanic, and Luigi Barzini, a journalist. These three resolute men had taken exactly 44 days to cover the whole distance, battling against adversities of every kind. This triumphant achievement for the Italians spurred on yet greater feats of endurance, and in 1908 a group of cars left the United States for the New York to Paris run of 21,760 miles. It was won by an American car, the 'Thomas Flyer'

Birth of an industry

In the early years of this century the automobile was developing quickly, from both the technical and the stylistic points of view. Single-cylinder engines gave way to more powerful and lighter ones with four or more cylinders. The 'horseless carriage' developed its own personality and soon a special bodywork was being built for it. This particular job was such a specialized one that car manufacturers would often deal just with the mechanical parts and leave the job of 'clothing' the car to the coach builders. In those formative years the names that are now so famous were born: Mercedes in 1901, Rolls Royce in 1904, Austin in 1905, Opel and Vauxhall to name only five. They were not without competition: Berliet, Lanchester, Laurin & Klement, Spyker, Gregoire and other companies that no longer exist also came into being at that time.

The year 1908 marked the end of the pioneering era and the beginning of the industrial one. This transformation was due to the revolutionary ideas of Henry Ford who introduced mass production methods. In that same year Ford brought out the famous Model T, the first car to be mass-produced, and, with slight modifications, 15 million of these cars were produced over the next 19 years. This was the vehicle whose simplicity of design, low cost and easy availability motorized the United States, and which became an example to manufacturers all over the world, who incorporated many of its features into their own production.

12

$1 39 6-Cylinder

An Instructive Toy

See the Engine in Motion

Large chauffeur-driven limousines evoke memories of the prohibition era. This model from a 1930 catalogue of Montgomery Ward & Co had a clockwork motor which moved the valves, fan and crankshaft.

A huge new industry was born as motor companies everywhere grew to be aware of the necessity of organized production on a modern basis. The factories expanded; the small workshops became large industries, and the skilled craftsmen had to give way to mass production. This industrial expansion was accompanied by considerable technical progress, and there were constant improvements and new and better inventions. One of the most far-reaching discoveries was the fact that power tends to increase as cylinder capacity decreases. Today there are cars with a 500, 800, 1000 or 1500 cc capacity, but at the beginning of the century cars with 5000, 6000 or even 7000 cc were regarded as perfectly normal. There were even monster racing cars with 30,000 cc engines, such as the champion Fiat 300 hp. The paradox was that while these gigantic engines consumed vast quantities of gasoline, they did not even approach the power of the smaller present-day engines. Technology solved this problem: cylinder capacity was reduced and so power was increased. Thus the utility car came into being. One of the first was the Fiat 'Zero', which was brought out in 1912, had an 1800 cc engine, and was already a great improvement over the previous 5700 cc Fiat 4. The same trend occurred in all the car-producing countries where light vehicles were mass-produced and sold at prices that were well within the reach of a large section of the public. In 1905 Peugeot brought out the 'AG', a little car with a 700 cc engine; then, in 1913, they launched an even tinier one called the 'Bébé', designed by Ettore Bugatti. These early utility cars were revived during the post-war years under the name of cycle cars.

Automobile engineering progressed in all fields: tires, brakes, shock-absorbers, and electrical systems were constantly being improved with a view to making the car more comfortable. In 1913 Lancia showed its Theta model, which was the first car in Europe to have a complete electrical system, consisting of ignition, lights and starter. Speed also increased at the same rate, and records were constantly being made, and then broken. In 1910 a speed of 130 mph had already been attained. Inevitably, enormous autodromes and special motor-racing circuits sprang up all over Europe and America, such as the one at Indianapolis which was constructed in 1909. Automobiles and drivers were tested to their limit on these circuits, battling to attain speeds of around 125 mph.

Then came the 1914-18 war, an event that was seriously to arrest progress in automobile engineering. But it was the first truly mechanized war and cars were to play an important role in it. The first significant event was the famous one concerning the 'Taxis of the Marne'. On the 7th September, as the German armed forces prepared to advance on Paris, the French General Gallieni requisitioned a thousand taxis from Paris, filled them with his troops and sent them to the border to contain the German advance into the Marne district. On all the battlefronts during the war, trucks and new vehicles, such as the armoured cars and tanks, were used in most military operations, while behind the lines the automobile factories were adapted for the production of military equipment.

When the war ended in 1918, the automobile was returned to its peacetime uses. But it had not passed through this great upheaval in vain, because wartime experiments had taught the motor industry a great deal. This was particularly true in America where the industry moved well ahead of its European counterparts. By this time another major manufacturer stood alongside Ford, the General Motors Company, formed in 1908 by William C. Durant. At first GMC incorporated Buick, Oldsmobile and Cadillac, and then other companies were absorbed. In 1916 even Chevrolet became a member of the new group, and about ten years later two European companies, Vauxhall and Opel, were also taken over by this huge American enterprise.

Once the adverse effects of the war began to diminish, the car industry on both sides of the Atlantic redoubled its activities. 1919 saw the Indianapolis 500-mile race, and the first post-war car show at Marseilles, France, which was closely followed by the Paris Show. In Italy the major event of the year was the advent of the new Fiat utility car, the '501' with a 1460 cc engine, a robust and economical vehicle designed for the mass market. In England the Austin and

6-01 Roadster

This colorful assortment of popular Roadsters immediately recommends this package of twelve pieces, consisting of three Buicks, with blue chassis and yellow body; three Cadillacs, with grey chassis and blue body; three Oldsmobiles, with red chassis and grey body; three Chevrolets with yellow chassis and red body.

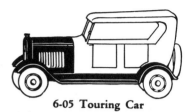

6-05 Touring Car

A box of surprising brilliance is this package of twelve Touring Cars with three Buicks, three Cadillacs, three Oldsmobiles, and three Chevrolets. (See Roadster for color combinations.)

Morris companies had been established in 1905 and 1912 respectively, and soon became very popular with motorists. The Cowley model was received enthusiastically and soon became regarded as the classic British car.

The main concern of all the manufacturers at the beginning of the 1920s was to produce small-cylinder cars, and so, as before the war, they made small fast cars known as 'cycle cars'. So the post-war years became the heyday for many firms such as Amilcar, Salmson, Peugeot and Austin.

The golden years

Perhaps the most phenomenal development of the post-war period, however, was that of Citroën. André Citroën was a businessman of great insight and considerable technical knowledge who looked forwards and saw the great potential for mass-produced cars aimed at a vast buying public. In 1920 he launched his '10 CV', which proved an immediate success. It had a 1500 cc engine and was a robust and yet elegant vehicle especially designed for the mass market. But the greatest success of all belonged to the little '5 CV' which was brought out in 1922.

1922 was also a memorable year for the Italian automobile trade, marked in particular by four important events: Milan held Italy's first post-war car show; Lancia brought out that extraordinary car called the Lambda; an autodrome was built in Monza in just three months; and in the field of racing Fiat achieved a magnificent victory at Strasbourg, when Nazzaro beat all other competitors at the wheel of the famous '804'. Next year at the Monza European Grand Prix yet another Fiat, this time driven by Salamano, won the coveted prize. Then in 1924 a Fiat competition car at that time called 'Mephistopheles', but today known by the name of its builder and driver – Elridge – made a record run at 145 mph on the measured track at Arpajon.

These were the golden years of automobile racing: Brooklands, Indianapolis, Targa Florio, the Grand Prix of France, Monza, Brescia, Montlhéry and Le Mans drew huge enthusiastic crowds to witness Ballot, Bugatti, Delage,

Duesenberg, Mercedes, Fiat and Sunbeam competing in breathtaking races. In the meantime, a new name had emerged in the racing world; that of Alfa Romeo. The company had started production in 1909, and for several years its cars had been competing on the race tracks, not winning any major trophies, but showing tremendous potential. At last, victory went to Alfa Romeo in the Targa Florio of 1923. For several years after that the famous eight-cylinder P2's dominated important international competitions. Among their most brilliant victories were the Lyons Grand Prix of 1924, with Campari at the wheel, and the Italian Grand Prix of the same year, won by Antonio Ascari.

Another influential name during the twenties was that of Ettore Bugatti, to whom automobile design owes a great deal. This determined and imaginative Italian emigrated to France shortly after he began experimenting with automobile design and there he first worked with De Dietrich and then Peugeot, gaining skill and experience before he set up his own company. He built racing car, family saloon and aircraft engines and his aim was to bring down the cylinder size as much as possible. His most successful creation was the Type 35, a racing car which, between 1924 and 1929, won more than a thousand competitions and was driven by the most famous racing drivers of the time. Bugatti, who spent most of his life either in the workshops or on the race-track, gradually formulated an idea that would be the ultimate in mechanical and aesthetic perfection. Thus, in 1927, the Royale, the most outstanding and exclusive of all custom-built vehicles, was born. Only seven were made and all were bought by celebrities.

Indeed, it is an important element in our story that the twenties were not only the age of mass-production for a large public, but also the era of extremely luxurious vehicles, in which refined details and technical perfection were the chief concerns of manufacturers such as Rolls Royce, Isotta Fraschini, Hispano Suiza, and later Duesenberg. Such cars went to kings, financial and industrial leaders, and movie stars. The automobile industry was soon to be

14

Facing page: Tootsietoy was one of the most successful firms of model makers in the 'thirties. Although factory-made, many of the models were accurate representations of individual automobile makes.

paralyzed by another world crisis – the Depression – but during the years that preceded it, development and expansion continued at a faster rate than ever before all over the world.

In America, after 20 years of good service, the famous Ford 'T' was succeeded by the Model 'A', which became another highly popular car. The public could choose from a wide range of automobiles of all kinds, but during the late twenties and early thirties Lincoln, Chevrolet, Cadillac, Buick, Chrysler, Pierce Arrow, Packard and the great Duesenbergs were the most fashionable cars.

Across the Atlantic, in Britain, motoring enthusiasts soon realized the quality of another make – Bentley – which was to win much fame in the sporting world. Between 1924 and 1930 their cars gained five victories at Le Mans, and in the 1929 race the first four places went to Bentleys.

In Italy, meanwhile, Fiat brought out a new car destined for the popular market (1925). This was the 990 cc '509' which became a great success, production continuing until 1929, along with other models of medium or large cylinder capacity.

1927 was another significant year for the sporting world: the first 'Mille Miglia' race was held across 1,000 miles of open Italian roads. Record runs were also made during 1927: on March 29th a Napier-Lion driven by Segrave attained a speed of 185 mph, another great event in the history of automobiles. In Italy Tazio Nuvolari, who had started a promising career in motorcycle racing, turned to motor cars and began his legendary progress to fame. Other racing drivers also rose to fame during this time. One of these was Alfieri Maserati who, with his two brothers, set up the famous factory of that name.

In spite of the impending economic crisis, 1928 brought a great many beautiful cars to the notice of the public. In Germany, Mercedes, fresh from their sporting successes, were preparing the elegant and powerful 'SS' and the '36/220' which would brighten the dark years to come. Meanwhile in Italy, Lancia brought out their Dilambda, while Alfa Romeo launched their '1500' which was later improved as the '1750'.

After the Depression

When the worst years of the Depression were over, the automobile industry all over the world slowly began to recover, and soon production was as active as ever. For instance, in Italy, a new Fiat was launched – another family car – the '508' or Balilla, and one year later a sports version, the '508-S', was made. From this the famous 'Coppa d'Oro' and the 'Mille Miglia' developed. Lancia too put on the market a beautiful and interesting vehicle, the 1200 cc Augusta, which was produced between 1933 and 1936. Alfa Romeo entered upon a period of great activity: it brought out such famous cars as the '1750', the '8c 2300' and the 'P 3', the last glorious Grand Prix winner they were to make before their official retirement from racing in 1933.

In France, Citroën, fresh from the world record they had achieved in 1933 on the Montlhéry with 'Rosalie', launched its '8 CV' which was given the same name. Renault, Peugeot and Delage brought out new models to meet the changing requirements of the market, and Voisin launched their powerful '22 CV'.

Meanwhile, in the States, the smaller companies, such as Pierce Arrow and Franklin, found it impossible to continue production. The large enterprises, however, survived the crisis and rose to greater heights. General Motors moved into the new field of the diesel engine, and Ford launched the first low-price V-8 in 1932.

But while the trend in the USA was towards greater concentration of the motor industry, in Britain, initially, at least, the reverse was true, for after the Depression there were six major companies – Ford, Morris, Vauxhall, Rootes, Austin and Standard – whereas in 1929 there had only been three.

We shall leave this history of the automobile in 1934, at a point when construction techniques, which had improved beyond all measure, continued to evolve, incorporating the ideas of car designers from all over the world. The old traditional body shapes and designs were on the point of giving way to streamlined ones, and the automobile could look forward to a great future.

15

1

69 is an important date in the history of the car: in that year a rather
y three-wheeled truck, invented by the French engineer Nicolas
ot, was able to travel a few dozen yards under its own power at what
en considered an incredible speed of 5 mph, thus fulfilling the dreams
ny brilliant men all over the world. Built almost entirely in wood, it was
with a large boiler at the front, a two-cylinder steam engine, and
wheel drive. A year later, on 20 November 1770 at Vincennes, Nicolas
ot tried out another more highly developed model which can still be
oday at the Conservatoire des Arts et Métiers in Paris (Precisia model,
1:32).

2 Throughout the nineteenth century, steam vehicles could be seen
manoeuvering, often with great difficulty, in the streets, and they became the
object of much curiosity, even hostility. Nevertheless, production continued,
the vehicles being known by the names of 'velocifers', steam coaches, drags
or trailers, and street trains. The latter were strongly opposed by the first
railway companies who finally succeeded in having a law passed to limit their
use. The model in the photograph is of a famous French steam automobile,
the Mancelle, which was completed in 1878. It was built by Amédée Bollée Sr,
a pioneer of motor construction. The engine was housed at the front, and the
boiler behind. The Mancelle could reach 25 mph (Rami Model, scale 1:43).

2

3

4

The two Germans Karl Benz and Gottlieb Daimler are universally recognized as the inventors of the internal combustion engine, since they were the first to patent their design. Between 1885 and 1886 the first vehicles with internal combustion engines were seen on the streets. The little model shown in the photograph is a reproduction of the famous 1885 Daimler. This was simply an open framework to which was attached a single-cylinder 462 cc engine (Wiking model, scale 1:43).

Unlike Daimler, Benz designed a special tricycle in which to mount his combustion engine. This vehicle made its first journey at Mannheim on July 1886, covering a short distance at a speed of 9 mph. The single-cylinder horizontal gasoline engine had a cylinder capacity of 980 cc. The Benz tricycle became the main attraction at the 1887 Paris Exhibition, and there were several offers to buy the patent (Wiking model, scale 1:43).

Karl Benz followed up this first success by presenting his 'Victoria' model to the public in 1893. It had a single-cylinder rear-mounted 2123 cc engine,

and in 1894 the driver Van Liebig gave it a test run from Reichenberg to Rheims and back, a journey of over a thousand miles (Dugu model, scale 1:43).

6 The names of Panhard and Levassor are among the most famous in the history of the automobile. In 1890 they made the prototype and a year later their dog cart, a model of which is shown here, appeared on the market. It had a 4 hp rear-mounted combustion engine (Europe Kit model, scale 1:32).

7 During the last years of the nineteenth century and the beginning of the twentieth, the steam engine was far more successful than the combustion engine, even in competitions. The photograph shows Scotte's 1892 steam automobile (Rami model, scale 1:43).

8 The first American automobile dates back to 1893 and was invented by the brothers Charles and Francis Duryea. In 1895 it won the first race to be held in America, from Chicago to Evanston, covering the distance of 49 miles in 10 hours 23 minutes (Gowland & Gowland model, scale 1:43).

9

10

On 19 December 1893 the *Petit Journal* sponsored the first competition for [horse]seless carriages'. The organizers did not actually use the word 'race', as [it] might have provoked an unfavourable reaction from the authorities and [the] public who were not yet used to such events. Thus, on 22 July 1894, the first [78-m]ile 'Paris-Rouen' race took place, and has since gone down in history as [bein]g the first motor race. Any type of automobile was allowed to run; they [coul]d be propelled by steam, electricity, gasoline, gas or oil. Of the 102 [vehi]cles that entered, 88 reached the semi-finals and 21 the finals. The fastest [tim]e was achieved by a De Dion & Bouton steam vehicle, driven by the [inve]ntors, at an average speed of 15 mph. However, it was judged to be [rath]er too bulky a machine, and was awarded only second prize, the first being [divi]ded between a Panhard & Levassor and a Peugeot. The photograph shows [the] winning De Dion & Bouton (Rio model, scale 1:43).

This little three-wheeled Bernardi invention, dating back to 1894, is a [goo]d example of the considerable effort the Italians made to design a functional [inter]nal combustion engine within a chassis. Unfortunately Professor [Bern]ardi's vehicles, which date back to 1883, did not meet with enough [succ]ess to make them really well known. The tri-car shown here had a [sing]le-cylinder rear-mounted 624 cc horizontal engine with water-cooling; [and], three-speed gears, chain transmission, and a top speed of 20 mph (Dugu [mod]el, scale 1:43).

Between 1885 and 1890 the first electric cars could be seen, but although [they] attracted a good deal of interest they were eventually replaced by the [gaso]line engine. An important milestone was the world record made in 1899 [by t]he Belgian Camille Jenatzy in an electric car called 'Jamais Contente' [(Ne]ver Content), the first to reach a speed of 60 mph. The model shown in [this] photograph is of the 1898 French Hauthier, described as 'an electric car [for] city use' (Rami model, scale 1:43).

Another pioneer of the automobile was the Frenchman, Armand [Peu]geot. From the time of the French Revolution the Peugeot family had been [well] known for its involvement with the metal industry. In 1885 the Peugeot [brot]hers started to build bicycles, and then Armand Peugeot, like Panhard [bef]ore him, bought the Daimler patent for the construction of combustion [eng]ines. Peugeot's name frequently appeared among those of the competitors [in t]he first automobile races; in fact, he was one of the moving forces behind [the] Paris-Rouen race. The photograph shows an elegant 1898 Peugeot coupé [(Pr]ecisia model, scale 1:32).

11

12

21

13

13 The 1899 Gobron Brillié is a typical example of the late nineteenth century 'horseless carriage'. It had a two-cylinder engine cooled by a coiled radiator system. It was brought into being in 1898 by Gustave Gobron and Eugéne Brillié and became the holder of a number of world speed records, including the record speed of 105 mph in 1904 (Precisia model, scale 1:32).

14 The photograph shows the first Fiat, the '$3\frac{1}{2}$ hp', which dates back to 1899. On 1 July of that year the firm of Fiat was founded in Turin on a starting capital of 800,000 lire. The new industry did not waste any time, and only a few months after the firm had been established, the new '$3\frac{1}{2}$ hp' was launched from the workshops at Corso Dante. Designed by the engineer Aristide Faccioli, this car was powered by a horizontal two-cylinder 679 cc engine; it was capable of a speed of 20 mph and had a gasoline consumption 30 mpg. (Model built by Silvio Morselli for the Fiat Historical Centre, scale 1:5).

14

15

The French firm of De Dion & Bouton was established in 1883 by the
[moto]r enthusiast Count Albert De Dion and a highly skilled mechanic
[name]d Georges Bouton, to produce steam vehicles. Six years later, they
[decid]ed to build gasoline-driven cars. In 1899 they produced their first 'vis-à-vis'
[(fac]e to face), which had a single-cylinder 499 cc engine. The extremely
[accu]rate model of this car shown here is the work of a well-known Italian
[spec]ialist who took several hundred hours to complete it. (Model constructed
[by C]arlo Brianza, scale 1:11).

16   Dissatisfied with a car he had bought, the American James Ward
Packard is said to have decided to build one for himself. This was in 1899 and
only four years later, in 1903, one of the most famous motor companies in the
world came into being, the Packard Motor Company. In the same year, the
pioneer driver Tom Fetch, driving a Packard which had been given the name
'Old Pacific', became the first man to drive across the United States, in only
61 days. The photograph shows a 1900 Packard. (Model built by Eduardo
Brazao, scale 1:43).

16

23

17

18

17 The name of Mercedes, which today is such a distinguished one in the field of automobile engineering, originated from a charming young German in the late nineteenth century. Emile Jellinek, who was the general manager Daimler at that time, put forward the idea that a pleasant-sounding girl's name would be far more appealing to the clients, and he suggested baptizing the Daimler cars with the name of his own daughter. The idea was greeted enthusiastically and so, in 1901, the company brought out its first Mercedes. The next year saw the debut of the four-cylinder Simplex, which was both fast and strong, combining the best qualities that could be found in a car at that time (Rio model, scale 1:43).

18 In 1901 Fiat produced its '12 hp' which even from an aesthetic point of view was a distinct improvement on the first Fiat. It was designed by the engineer Giovanni Enrico who by that time had succeeded Faccioli as technical director of the firm. Between 1901 and 1902 about one hundred of these cars were produced, and they became the first Fiats to be sold abroad. Initially, the '12 hp' was fitted with a coiled radiator but this was then replace by the more functional honeycomb type. It had a four-cylinder 3770 cc engin and could travel at 45 mph. When challenged by Panhard to a 185-mile race the Villanova-Bologna road on 24 November 1902, the Fiat beat, and put ou of the race, both rival cars (Rio model, scale 1:43).

19 1902 was the golden year for endurance tests on the open road. Especia in France, very long races were organized that proved strenuous tests of both men and machines. The difficult roads, unreliable cars, lack of assistance and often the hostility of local inhabitants turned these competitions into exhausting and dangerous adventures. The Paris-Vienna race is a particularly famous one: 137 competitors started the course on 22 June but the crossing o the mountainous Swiss border proved too much for nearly all the entrants, and put most of the favourites out of the race. To everyone's surprise, the winner was Marcel Renault in his little 16 hp vehicle bearing the number 147 He had beaten all the others at the almost incredible average of 39 mph. The photograph shows the winning Renault (Safir model, scale 1:43).

20 The photograph shows a curious 1902 English racing car known as the 'General'. The unusual wedge shape of this Grand Prix vehicle is the result of the designer's commendable attempt to give it a streamlined shape. Unfortunately, however, the relatively low speed of cars at those times – around 60 mph – made such ideas somewhat premature. The 'General', powered by a 40 hp Buchet engine, did not take part in any races and remained at the experimental stage (Rio model, scale 1:43).

21 The emblem and name of Vauxhall, one of the first British motor companies, originated in the Middle Ages, during the reign of William the Conqueror. Almost a thousand years later, the Vauxhall Iron Works was opened and the company concentrated on ship-building, until 1903 when the built their first automobile. It was a small vehicle with a single-cylinder 970 cc engine, and an unusual pointed hood (Guiterman model, scale 1:32).

19

20

21

22

23

24

22 Henry Ford was born in 1862, of a farming family. From his childhood he had been fascinated by mechanical things, and so his first job was repairing watches. Then he turned his attention to steam vehicles. His father was not very enthusiastic about these activities, but young Ford was determined to succeed; he settled in Detroit and found a job with Westinghouse. After working in the factory during the daytime, he spent his nights constructing a car in a little laboratory he had set up for himself. In 1896 he completed a four-wheeled vehicle with a gasoline-powered engine. Three years later, after he and his partners had gathered some capital, he founded the Detroit Automobile Company only to leave it shortly afterwards. At last in 1903, with money earned as a racing driver, he was able to achieve his dream; the Ford Motor Company was born. From that time on, an ever-increasing number of Ford's cars was to be seen. The photograph shows a 1903 Ford. (This model was built by Eduardo Brazao, scale 1:43).

23–24 The French Darracq was built in 1895 by Alessandro Darracq, a bicycle-maker. The first vehicles of this type appeared at the end of the centur and gained considerable fame, due mainly to their brilliant racing achievemen which included the world speed records in both 1904 and 1905. In 1905, Darracq extended his activities to Italy and opened a factory in Milan, and a few years later the Alfa was released to the public. The photographs show two views of an excellent scale model of the 1904 Darracq. (Model made by Manuel Olive Sans, scale 1:20).

26

25

The first American Oldsmobiles were known as curved dash cars ...use of their distinguished curved fronts which characterized them from ...r cars for a few years. One of these small cars, fitted with a 1563 cc engine, ...exhibited at the automobile show in New York, after travelling there from ...roit under its own power in seven and a half days. (Model made by ...ardo Brazao, scale 1:43).

26 The French firm of Delahaye made cars from 1894 to 1954. Originally, the company had built machines for manufacturing matches, but Emile Delahaye was among the first to see the great potential offered by the new means of transport. His company began to build cars and he was soon to achieve considerable success. The picture shows one of the 1904 versions (Rami model, scale 1:43).

26

27

28

In 1900, the first Dutch car – the Spyker – was launched. The company based in Amsterdam, and in 1902 it became the first to build six-cylinder es. They ceased production in 1925. The car in the picture is a 1905 er with a 2546 cc engine; the characteristic rounded radiator grill is just e (Lesney model, scale 1:47).

In 1885 Edoardo Bianchi opened a bicycle workshop in Milan, but this ious businessman soon became fascinated by the idea of building nobiles, and at the end of the century he started producing cars as well as les. A prototype appeared in 1899 and then in 1903 he brought out the ton'. Three years later he made his first really successful car: this was 5/20 hp' vehicle shown in the photograph. It was sometimes called the t springs' (Rio model, scale 1:43).

Early twentieth century records frequently mention De Dion & Bouton, tors of the 'De Dion rear axle arrangement' which replaced chain mission. This system was tried out on the Peking-Paris run, in which two Dion & Bouton cars took part, both based on their model 'G'. This r model, which came out in 1907 and had a small 942 cc engine, is shown e photograph. (Model made by Mario Grossi, scale 1:12).

In 1904 Charles Stewart Rolls, son of an English peer and a brilliant eer driver, had already built one motor car of some renown. At the same , Henry Royce, a skilled engineer, was experimenting with motors of his design in a small workshop in the suburbs of London. Realizing that they so much in common, they went into partnership, founding the legendary s Royce company. A year later, in 1905, the new firm had already pleted several large motors and shortly afterwards they presented that car to the public. This was the famous 'Silver Ghost', so-called because s six-cylinder 7400 cc engine which was almost silent compared with e of other cars of the day. A real masterpiece of perfection, it came on the ket in 1907 (Lesney model, scale 1:47).

One of the most outstanding events in the history of the automobile was Peking-Paris run which took place in 1907. The Paris newspaper *Le Matin* the originator and sponsor of the race, which started on 10 June in Peking five cars competing. After 44 days on the road, an Itala made by ghese, Guizzardi and Barzini, crossed the finishing line, a month ahead of other competitors. The 35/45 hp Itala shown in the photograph had a 3 cc engine (Rio model, scale 1:43).

32 Fiat, like the other big companies, did not hesitate to take part in the first competitive events since these not only proved to be excellent testing grounds for the cars, but also brought the company's name to the attention of the public. In 1907 the 130 hp Fiat was entered for its first races: this powerful racing car had a 16,285 cc engine and was capable of a speed of about 100 mph. On 2 July the French Automobile Club Grand Prix was held at Dieppe and the 'limited consumption car' category was introduced: the cars could be of any cylinder capacity but could not have a gasoline consumption of over 9 mpg. Thirty-seven vehicles from six different countries competed in the race and after a series of dramatic incidents, Felice Nazzaro crossed the winning line in his 130 hp Fiat, bearing the number F.2, at an average speed of 70 mph. The reproduction of the 1907 130 hp Fiat shown in the picture was made by an Italian model maker. (Model made by Carlo Brianza, scale 1:13).

33 The picture above shows a detail of the 1907 hp Fiat. As can be seen, this model accurately reproduces not only the superficial features of the car, but also all the mechanical details. (Model made by Carlo Brianza, scale 1:12).

34

In 1908 Henry Ford introduced mass-
production methods into his factories and launched
his famous Model 'T' which was soon to
revolutionize the entire automobile industry and
take America into the motor age. The individual
parts of the Model 'T' were pre-fabricated and so
could be put together on an assembly line. With
this ingenious idea, Ford was successful beyond all
expectations, putting all his competitors completely
out of the running. The Model 'T', with its four-
cylinder 2900 cc engine, was strong, simple and
functional. Fifteen million examples of this
automobile were built and it stayed in production
for 20 years without any substantial changes.
Nearly all the Model 'T's which came out of the
Ford works were black, as this facilitated repairs
and the matching of spare parts. Henry Ford used
to joke: 'Our clients can choose any colour they
like, so long as it's black' (Corgi Toys model,
scale 1:43).

Fiat soon became interested in the production
of small and medium capacity cars in addition to
their more powerful models, and in 1908 they began
work on a low cylinder capacity car. This was the
7/24 hp model, with a four-cylinder 4500 cc engine,
which could carry four to six people and was
capable of a speed of 35 to 40 mph. The model of
this car shown on the right accurately reproduces
every detail, such as the radiator, headlights, and
suspension. (Made by Mario Grossi, scale 1:12).

36 The photograph shows a detail of the 1908
Fiat illustrated above, revealing the engine and
driving seat. Here again, a great many tiny details
can be seen and it is these, the result of many days
work, which give the model such value and realism.
(Model made by Mario Grossi, scale 1:12).

37 The big racing events at the beginning of the
century had some really outstanding Mercedes cars
competing in them. One of the most spectacular
victories was seen at the fourth Gordon Bennett
races which took place in Ireland in 1903. It was
in this year that Mercedes had all their competition
cars destroyed by fire a day before the race, but
still won it with one of their mass-produced cars
driven by the great Camille Jenatzy. The following
year, at Ostende, Mercedes set the world speed
record at 95 mph. Another important race for this
German company was the French Automobile
Club Grand Prix at Dieppe in 1908, when the
Mercedes driver, Lautenschlager, surpassed all his
rivals with an average speed of 70 mph. The
photograph shows the winning 1908 Mercedes at
Dieppe (Lesney model, scale 1:48).

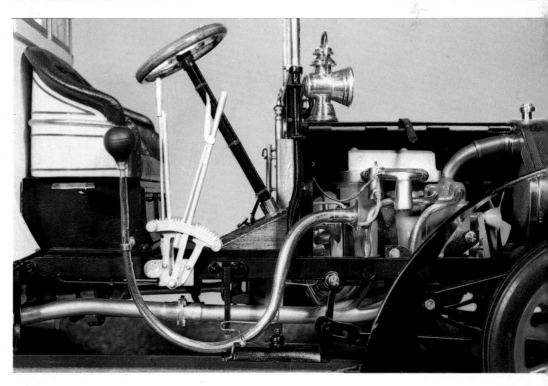

38

39

While people were still talking about the great success of Borghese, ...zardi and Barzini's Itala, another sensational event became headline ... This was the New York-Paris run, covering 25,000 miles and once again ...ized by the newspaper *Le Matin*. At 10 am on 18 February 1908, in front ...ousands of spectators, six cars lined up on Fifth Street, for the start of the ... This amazing marathon took the competitors across the United States to ...rancisco, and then through Alaska and into Siberia. Several alterations ... be made to the course, and after adventures of every kind and the ... of the Nordic winters, the only car to succeed in completing the course ...d triumphant in Paris waving the Stars and Stripes. The winner was a ...as Flyer and the date was 30 July of the same year. The photograph shows ...inning car (Rio model, scale 1:43).

...n 1905 the British firm Austin came into being, created by Herbert ...n who had been working with Wolseley since 1895. The first car of interest ...e little Austin Seven, the ancestor of the many future generations of ... cars that were to have such great success. It came out in 1909 and was ...st four-cylinder car to be mass-produced in Britain. Specialization in low ...er capacity cars did not prevent Austin from making larger cars, such as ... hp model which was produced between 1906 and 1914. The photograph ...s a 40 hp 1908 model. (Model made by Eduardo Brazao, scale 1:43).

...During the first ten years of this century, great progress was made in the ...mobile industry, particularly in Italy where 96 car factories were opened, ...ugh very few of them are now in existence. In 1906 the F.I.A.L. (the ...viation of Fabbrica Italiana Automobile Legnano) was established in ...wn of Legnano. Two years later, their first 'A 6/8 hp' model was brought ...t was powered by a two-cylinder 1135 cc engine, and had three forward ... and one reverse. Its pleasing rounded lines and relatively low cost ...d to make it a very popular car (Dugu model, scale 1:43).

...Another enterprise which changed from bicycle making to automobile ...ruction was the German company owned by Adam Opel. They bought ...atents from Lutzmann, a pioneer German car firm, and having become ...ent for the French firm, Darracq, they began building cars for the ...on Bennett Races Cup in 1904. Achieving success with these cars, they ...d to construct their own model. One of the most successful was the ...) model, known as 'Doktor', which came out in 1909. Following the ...ion of the Opel company, the 4/8 hp was not a fast car; but it was solid, ...nd reliable (Lesney model, scale 1:46).

40

41

33

42

43

42 The 1909 Lanchester, the original landau with an outside driver's seat, is a fine example of the traditional British car. Lanchester was the first firm to build cars in Britain. The company was founded in 1896 and immediately distinguished itself by the originality of its technical skill. The 20 hp vehicle shown in the photograph had such interesting features as a wick carburettor, preselector gear change, a tiller-type steering mechanism and disc brakes (Airfix model, scale 1:32).

43 Steam-powered automobiles survived far longer in the United States than elsewhere. The Stanley was one of the last examples of the steam vehicle. It had a truly brilliant career, and its name is entered in the Golden Book of speed records, because in 1906 a Stanley reached 120 mph, and later 126 mph. This is a 1909 Stanley Steamer (Revell model, scale 1:32).

44 The search for new inventions and ideas that would give a car originality has from time to time led coach-builders to produce rather

extravagant designs. Examples of this in the past include the tri-berline sho[w] in the photograph which was built by Grégoire in 1910. It was presented at [the] Paris Fair and the bodywork was signed by two famous coach-makers of th[e] time, Alin and Liautard. This imposing vehicle, which echoed the style of t[he] old diligences, had many features designed to make a long journey as comfortable as possible, and among its sumptuous trimmings there were quilted velvet upholstery, lace trimmings and little curtains at the windows (Safir model, scale 1:43).

45 The French firm Berliet was founded by Marius Berliet, an enterprisin[g] businessman. The company, which is now known for its heavy vehicles, beg[an] producing automobiles in Lyons in 1898. It soon had such a high reputatio[n] that only a few years later, the President of the Republic, Raymond Poincaré, chose a Berliet as his official car. Several Berliets were entered in[to] motor races, and in 1910 a 40 hp model won an important event at Bologn[a]. The photograph shows a 1910 Berliet (Vieux Tacots model, scale 1:24).

34

44
45

35

46

46 In 1911 Fiat's Golden Book of records was enriched by yet another prize, won by Bruce Bro at the wheel of a 'S.74' Fiat which reached an average of almost 75 mph in the America Grand Prix, held that year at Savannah. This car had an engine that was capable of a maximum speed of 100 mph. With a capacity of 14,000 cc, it was a truly spectacular model, and fully loaded it weighed over 3400 lbs. A vehicle of the same typ took part in the French Grand Prix during the same year and came second, driven by Wagner. (Model made by Silvio Morselli for the Fiat Historical Centre, scale 1:15).

47 1912 was an important year for Fiat; in that year their 12–15 hp model, better known as 'Zero was launched. This vehicle is significant because, with its 1800 cc engine, it can be considered as the first utility passenger car. The 'Zero' was a great improvement on past cars and, even though it was not acceptable to all tastes, it opened up new possibilities to the automobile industry. The 'Zero' was also the first to have Fiat chassis and body work and was put on the market as the toure version. Later, the two-seater sports version and the landaulet were made by various coach-builder Other distinguishing characteristics of this car include a gas consumption of 20 mph, a speed of 40 mph, and three passenger seats. Two thousand 'Zeros' were put on the market between 1912 and 1915, a fact all the more exceptional when one considers that mass-production methods had yet to be introduced (Rio model, scale 1:43).

47

36

48 In 1906 Matteo Ceirano, a pioneer of automobile engineering and one of the founders of the Itala company, formed his own company in Turin and called it SPA (short for Societa Piedmontese Automobili). This firm, which was later to become famous for its trucks, made many beautiful cars and also had considerable success in the racing world. During the Libyan war and later in the First World War, the SPA trucks were distinguished by their high efficiency and great strength. When the war ended, the Turin factory produced several cars that rivalled those of other famous makers in their elegance of style and their high performance. The photograph shows a 1912 SPA sports version (Rami model, scale 1:43).

49 From the time of its inception until the present day, the British Rolls Royce company has maintained a tradition of stately and supreme elegance, which has made their cars the choice of royalty and wealthy people in the public eye, all over the world. These famous automobiles are still called by imaginative and appropriate names, such as 'Ghost', Phantom', 'Cloud', as reminders of their almost silent engines. They have always presented a great challenge to even the most famous coach-builders. Virtually travelling sitting-rooms, Rolls Royces are famous for all the comforts they provide, which make journeys so pleasant. Models are often constructed in accordance with the individual requirements of the clients. The Rolls Royce in the picture is a 1912 model, a masterpiece of elegance (Corgi Toys model, scale 1:43).

50 The British Daimler company was founded in 1893 with a view to using the Daimler patents in Great Britain. After a complete reorganization of the company in 1896, they concentrated on the construction of luxury cars, but their ambitious plans were not to become reality, and in 1911 Daimler went into partnership with the Birmingham Small Arms Company. However, during those eighteen years the factory had produced some attractive cars, such as the 1913 model shown in the photograph. (Model made by Eduardo Brazao, scale 1:43).

37

52   53

51   The Alfa company came into being in 1909 on the initiative of a group of automobile pioneers from Milan. Having obtained a loan from the Banca Agricola of Milan, they took over the workshops which Darracq had opened in Milan in 1906. From the outset, Alfa entered the racing world and their cars were clearly intended for this purpose. In 1913 the Italian coach-builder Castagna designed an unconventional tapering body which had been commissioned from him by Mario Ricotti. This unusual shape which the French call *trompe le vent* (wind deceiver), and we call streamlined, is one of the first examples of an aerodynamic body. (This shape becomes more and more important as the speed of the car increases.) The engine and mechanical components were made by Alfa, and so this car is now known as the Alfa Ricotti. It had a four-cylinder 4084 cc engine and was capable of a speed of 85 mph. (Model made by Michele Conti, scale 1:11).

52   The photograph shows the front view of the Alfa Ricotti. The emblem, trade name, headlights and honeycomb radiator, so beautifully reproduced, are only some of the accurate details of this miniature which was built in metal, with rubber tires. (Model made by Michele Conti, scale 1:11).

53   The 1913 Peugeot 'Bébé' shown in the photograph occupies a place of particular importance in the history of automobiles for two main reasons: it was designed by the great engineer Ettore Bugatti, and it is considered to be one of the first true saloon cars. A native of Italy, Ettore Bugatti went to France at an early age, and here in 1910 he set up his first workshop at Molsheim. At that time Bugatti was also working for Peugeot and created the little car which, because of its low cylinder capacity, was given the name Bébé. Its four-cylinder 856 cc engine could reach a speed of 40 mph, with a relatively low gasoline consumption; and it was immediately acclaimed as a masterpiece of engineering (Vieux Tacots model, scale 1:32).

38

54 William Richard Morris, who later became Lord Nuffield, was already running a successful bicycle and motor factory in the early twentieth century, but, like many other businessmen of his day, he was soon attracted by the possibility of building cars. In 1913 he completed the first Morris car, named the Oxford, which had a four-cylinder 1018 cc engine (Dinky Toys model, scale 1:43).

55 A French explorer called Antoine de la Mothe Cadillac went to America in 1701, and founded the city of Detroit; he never could have guessed that two centuries later his name would be given to a make of automobile. This came about in 1902 when Mr Henry Leland decided to open his own company in competition with Ford, and named it the Cadillac Automobile Company. Shortly afterwards, the first Cadillacs came on the market and soon became famous for their distinctive style and elegance. The photograph shows a 1913 Cadillac (Lesney model, scale 1:46).

56 For many years the pointed radiator was a distinctive feature of Mercedes cars, even in competition models such as the famous Grand Prix Mercedes that won at Lyons on 4 July 1914. The Mercedes tourer shown in the photograph was made during the same period (Revell model, scale 1:32).

55

56

39

On 7 September 1914 the First World War broke out, and the automobile
...oon to play a vital role on the battlefields. The way in which this happened
...w famous: the Germans broke through the French line and it became
...ous that they would soon invade Paris. Action had to be taken quickly, so
...rench General Gallieni requisitioned a thousand Paris taxis to carry fresh
...s to the Marne to contain the advance of the enemy. His quick thinking
...d the day: the Germans were forced back and the counter-offensive that
...wed resulted in the victorious Battle of the Marne. The triumphant 'taxis
...e Marne' were 1910 AG Renaults which had two-cylinder 1206 cc engines
...eat strength. There is no doubt that the high quality of these cars enabled
... to fulfil their mission so effectively (Rio model, scale 1:43).

At about the time that the First World War was about to break out in
...pe, the automobile industry in the United States was expanding rapidly.
...ddition to the big companies, many smaller ones also came into existence,
... even though some of them were to disappear in future years, they still have
...nportant place in the history of American vintage cars. Among them was
...irm owned by Harry Stutz who brought out his first car in 1911. It gave a
... performance in the Indianapolis race, bringing fame to both the car and its
...er. But the most successful model of all was the great 'Bearcat' which came
...n 1914. This stylish sports car had an engine with four cylinders in two
...ks; with its 6400 cc capacity it vied with the other 'monster' cars of its day
...eeds of over 80 mph. The Stutz firm survived until 1935 but was never
...n to produce such spectacular cars as the 'Bearcat' (Revell model, scale
...).

Antique-car enthusiasts tend to separate English cars into three categories:
...eran (up until 1904), Edwardian (from 1905 to 1916), and Vintage (1919
...930). The 1913 four-litre Vauxhall, called 'Prince Henry', which is shown in
...photograph, is an example of an Edwardian car. An elegant English
...er, it had a four-cylinder 3969 cc engine capable of withstanding even
...ng conditions, and a top speed of 75 to 80 mph (Lesney model, scale 1:45).

Vincenzo Lancia, a former Fiat racing driver, founded his famous
...omobile company in 1901. At first Lancia concentrated on low-powered
..., but a few years later they began to build larger engines, such as the
...2 'model 61'. After a few slight modifications the '61' gave way to the
...ous 'Theta' which was the first really important Lancia car and which
...odied several technical innovations. For example, it was the first European
...with a full electrical system. Its 4940 cc four-cylinder engine gave a top
...ed of 75 mph. After the 'Theta', which is shown in the photograph, came two
...ous World War I military vehicles, the 'Jota' and the 'Diota' (Dugu model,
...e 1:43).

61

62

61 The American Mercer company started in 1903 and was active for over 30 years, until 1935. Though it is not among the most famous automobile companies, it had its moment of glory in 1915 when the '35 Raceabout' was produced. This was a powerful racing car with a 4900 cc engine capable of a speed of 80 mph. It was a highly sought-after vehicle even at that time, and along with the Stutz it became an exceptional prize for connoisseurs; today the Mercer is among the most valuable of vintage cars. Few people were able to own a Mercer because the little factory was only able to produce a small number of vehicles a year. In 1912 a Mercer came third in the famous Indianapolis race, and the following year the car took second place. The scale model of the 1915 '35 Raceabout' shown in the photograph is the work of a well-known Spanish model maker whose name often appears in the specialized magazines of the model car world and whose models have contributed to a great many exhibitions. (Model made by Manuel Olive Sans, scale 1:20).

62 The photograph shows a detail of the model of the Mercer illustrated above. The central part of the car is full of details which the model maker has accurately and fully reproduced with extreme skill and precision. The brake and gear levers, the pedals, headlights, horn, gas tank and steering wheel are only some of these features. The model can be steered and has a fully operative suspension. Also of note are the folding circular windshield, the leather strap with a metal buckle which holds the hood in place and the tires with the original tread pattern. (Model made by Manuel Olive Sans, scale 1:20).

63

Less than one year after the end of World War I, Fiat brought out a new [med]ium-capacity car, the '501'. Designed by Carlo Cavalli, it combined good [perf]ormance with a reasonable price and low gas consumption. Between 1919 [and] 1926, Fiat built 65,000 of these cars which achieved great success both in [Italy] and abroad. The main characteristics of the '501' were the four-cylinder [1460] cc engine, four-speed gears, a gas consumption of over 20 mpg, and a [spee]d of 43 mph. It was available in tourer, sports and sedan versions. (Model [mad]e by Silvio Morselli for the Fiat Historical Centre, scale 1:5).

64 The famous Indianapolis racing circuit was inaugurated in 1909, and two years later the first 500-mile race was held, and it is still run annually. This race has often been most spectacular and has also been the scene of many accidents, some of them very tragic ones. It was the first sporting event to be restarted after the First World War, in 1919. The following year the race was won by Gaston Chevrolet driving the Monroe Special shown in the photograph (Aurora model, scale 1:32).

64

43

65

66

67

68

At the beginning of the twenties, the British firm of Morris followed up its [pre]-war success with the Oxford by bringing out the new Cowley with a [dist]inctive 'bullnose' front. This was a reasonably priced, medium-capacity car, [with] a four-cyinder 1550 cc engine which was capable of a speed of 50 mph [Air]fix model, scale 1:32).

The French Automobile Club Grand Prix run in Strasbourg on 16 July [192]2 was the scene of the noteworthy victory of a '804' Fiat driven by Felice [Na]zzaro. Built in accordance with the new formula brought out that same year, [it h]ad a capacity of less than the two litres, weighed 1625 lbs and could reach [a sp]eed of 105 mph. The same vehicle met with yet further success at the Italia[n Gr]and Prix at Monza, when '804' Fiats came first and second. (Model made [by]Bruno Reggiani for the Fiat Historical Centre, scale 1:5).

Among the many events and new initiatives that came about immediately [afte]r the war, the advent of the Citroën company was of major importance in [the]history of the automobile. The engineer André Citroën, a man of great [inv]entiveness and organizational ability, had been at the head of a large [mu]nitions industry. In 1919 he decided to turn to automobile construction and [soo]n launched his first vehicle. Thanks to an extremely competitive price, its [suc]cess was beyond all expectations; but even this did not match the enormous [suc]cess that the 1922 Citroën model was to have. This was the famous 5 hp [Tr]efle' (Clover-leaf) which had a boat-shaped body and a lively 855 cc engine, [and] which is shown in the photograph (France Jouets model, scale 1:16).

In the post-war period there were about thirty automobile factories in [Ital]y. Among these was the Ansaldo Company which, by producing a massive [am]ount of military material, had played a decisive role in the victory of 1918. [The]y opened a factory in Turin for the construction of civilian vehicles and the [ph]otograph shows the Ansaldo '6c' which was brought out in 1922, and had a [190]0 cc six-cylinder engine (Dugu model, scale 1:43).

The Renault brothers, who were enthusiastic motorists, excellent [tec]hnicians and fearless racing drivers, opened their factory in 1898 and [sta]rted making the fast little cars that were to have such success in the [co]mmercial and racing worlds. During World War I, Renault made armoured [tan]ks. During the post-war period they brought out their '40 hp', which was in [pro]duction from 1923 until 1927. Its large 9123 cc engine enabled it to win two [wo]rld records: two 24-hour runs at averages of 85 and 105 mph. The photograph [sho]ws a 1923 '40 hp' Renault (Rio model, scale 1:43).

69

45

70

71

72

70 The impressive record-breaking racing car in the photograph was originally given the name of 'Mephistopheles', but it is better known as the Fiat-Eldridge. On 12 July 1924 at Arpajon in France it established a new world speed record with an average speed of 145 mph. This car was built by the Englishman Sir Ernest Eldridge using the body of a 1908 'SB.4' in which he fitted a First World War aircraft engine, the 'A.12b', to replace the original one which had been destroyed during a race. He drove the car to fame during this record-breaking run. The engine had a cylinder capacity of 21,706 cc and 320 hp. The model car shown here took a thousand hours to make. (Model made Carlo Brianza, scale 1:12).

71 It would be impossible to list the innumerable victories that Alfa Romeo has gained, and the legendary exploits of all its championship cars on the road and circuits of the world, from 1909 onwards. The twenties were a particularly successful period for this Italian company, but 1924 could be considered the golden year, due mainly to the 'P.2' designed by the engineer Vittorio Jano. In that year, with Giuseppe Campari at the wheel, this amazing car gained a brilliant victory at the Lyons Grand Prix, establishing the record speed of an average of 105 mph. The following year, the same car had a series of successes culminating in the winning of the world championship when it was driven by Gastone Brilli Peri (C.I.J. model, scale 1:10).

46

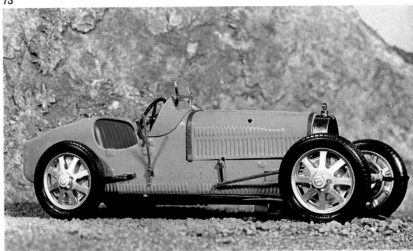

Industry was adversely affected for many years in Germany after the
[...] in World War I, and obviously took far longer than other European
[...]prises to recover in the post-war period. In spite of this, however, some
[...]cars were produced during the twenties and among them was the excellent
[...] 'Laubfrosch 3/12'. It was brought out in 1924, before Opel was
[...]porated with General Motors, and was one of the first utility cars to be
[...] produced. This was a little car, very similar to the French 5 hp Citroën
[...]h was much in vogue at that time. Its cylinder capacity was under 1000 cc
[...]t had outstanding durability and low running costs (Gama model, scale
[...].

Having spent the 1914-1918 war years designing aviation engines,
[...]re Bugatti returned to cars and in 1920 gained a victory at Le Mans.
[...]ever, it was four years later that he produced his real masterpiece, the
[...]e 35', which was to win over a thousand races and become the talk of the
[...]e racing world with its legendary duels with the most sophisticated cars
[...]e time, such as the Alfa Romeo, Delage and Mercedes. The 'Type 35'
[...]atti shown in the photograph had an eight-cylinder 1990 cc engine. Later, it
[...]fitted with a supercharger and called the '35 A'. Between 1926 and 1930
[...]35 B' and 'C', both with a more powerful 2261 cc engine plus supercharger,
[...]peted on the race track (Monogram model, scale 1:24).

The photograph shows a detail of the 1924 Isotta Fraschini '8/A' sports
[...]llustrated below. The maker of this miniature has accurately reproduced
[...]doors, hood and trunk (all of which can be opened), windows which slide,
[...] and front lights which function, working steering and suspension, padded
[...]s covered in leather, in addition to the detailed construction of the engine.
[...]del made by Giuseppe Da Corte, scale 1:8).

The Isotta Fraschini company, which was formed in Milan in 1899 by
[...]re Isotta and Vincenzo Fraschini, has an exciting and highly successful
[...]ory. Initially, the new company had wanted merely to be agents for
[...]ault, but soon the founders decided to manufacture their own cars. Thus
[...] born a generation of high-class vehicles, which had particular success in
[...] 1920-30 period, competing with the world's biggest motor names for
[...]ance and mechanical perfection. So the name of Isotta Fraschini became
[...]onymous with regality; sovereigns, finance and industrial magnates and
[...]er famous and wealthy people bought these sumptuous vehicles whose
[...]ywork was designed by the most highly respected designers of the time.
[...] model '8/A' which came out in 1924 was a marvellous vehicle with an
[...]t-cylinder 7372 cc engine. The high-quality bodywork of the sports version,
[...]ch was designed by Cesare Sala, can be seen in the photograph. (Model
[...]le by Giuseppe Da Corte, scale 1:8).

76 Fifteen million cars in 20 years – this says enough of the phenomenal success of the Ford 'T' which stayed in production, with only minor modifications, from 1908 until 1927. The 1925 Ford 'T' is shown in the photograph. Such features as its shape (which today may seem rather clumsy) and typical white tires evoke scenes from the old films of the twenties (A.M.T. model, scale 1:25).

77 In 1922 Lancia put their amazing Lambda on the market, and between 1922 and 1931 nine different versions were built. Of a somewhat higher quality than the average car of the time, it was a truly original vehicle incorporating several new technical improvements. For example, it was the first mass-produced car to have stressed coachwork and brakes on all four wheels. The four-cylinder 2123 cc engine was capable of a speed of over 70 mph. The photograph shows a 1925 Series V Lambda (Dugu model, scale 1'43).

78 The photograph shows another Panhard & Levassor – a 1925 '35 hp'. The company first decided to build this model in 1920, wishing to produce a high-class vehicle that would challenge all their competitors. This is the city coupé version with a 6500 cc engine (Solido model, scale 1:43).

79 The Fiat '509' was a most sensational car. It was shown at the 1925 Milan Automobile Show and was such a success that the factory was able to produce and sell nearly 100,000 models. The '509' was the typical passenger car of the twenties, with its 990 cc engine giving a gas consumption of 30 mph and a speed of approximately 50 mph. It was made in several versions, of which the one illustrated here is the tourer. The model is made in metal, the doors can be opened, the steering works, and the windshield is adjustable. (Model made by Gualtiero De Stavola, scale 1:20).

76

77

78

79

80

81

80 Citroën, in spite of having entered the automobile market about twenty years later than the other big manufacturers, soon made up for lost time. Having found success with their 5 hp, they brought out another car of quite revolutionary design, the 'B 2', which was to consolidate their fame. It was made in 1925 and was built entirely in steel. During that time, two more events brought Citroën into the limelight: the Sahara Crossing and the Black Cross Run, made by a half-tracked 'B 2'. The photograph shows an all-steel 1925 'B 2' (Rami model, scale 1:43).

81 Hispano Suiza, Isotta Fraschini and Rolls Royce were the three big names in the automobile industry in the twenties. In 1904, in Barcelona, a Swiss engineer, Birkigt, who had formerly been a railroad technician, opened an automobile factory which he called

50

ano Suiza. Success came quickly, especially
e race track, but it was mainly in the post-war
od, after this Swiss-Spanish enterprise had
ed to France, that it had the greatest success
its sensational vehicles. Equipped with
erful engines with 6 to 12 cylinders and a
city of up to 12,000 cc, they represented the
ate in luxury and quality. The model shown in
hotograph was made in 1926 (Solido model,
1:43).

Today, utility passenger cars are a
monplace, but 50 years ago the term had not
been coined. Even so, if one looks carefully
gh into the history of cars, a few ancestors of
nini-car can be found. For example, there was
German Hanomag 'Kommisbrot', which was
ght out in 1926 but caused more amusement
interest in its minute size. Driven by a small
engine, its shape and size had resulted in it
g given its German name which means
ier's bread roll' (Ziss RW model, scale 1:43).

Not content with his sporting triumphs, Ettore
atti, whose name had by now become a myth,
ded to build a really extraordinary car – a car,
ike of which had never been seen before and
h would be quite unbeatable. This ambitious
ect successfully came to fruition as the
chless masterpiece known as the Royale. Only
n Royales were built, four of which were sold to
ning monarchs. Orders poured in, in spite of the
nomical price, but Bugatti seemed to take
sure in refusing them. There were to be seven
ales and no more. They had a formidable
60 cc engine, a speed of over 123 mph and a
of about $40,000, which is evidence enough of
huge prestige. The photograph shows a detail
e 1927 Type 41 Bugatti Royale engine, which
housed in a body made by Weinberger. This
oduction was made by a well-known model
er who has made a faultless scale copy of the
nal car owned by the Vice Chairman of
eral Motors. (Model made by Giuseppe Da
e, scale 1:8).

This model of the Bugatti Royale is about two
long and is packed with the most magnificent
ils: the doors and trunk can be opened, the
ing works and the windows can be wound
n; the door handles have locks, there are lights,
ar is sprung and the horn can be sounded.
del made by Giuseppe Da Corte, scale 1:8).

85

86

85 1928 was the year in which the magnificent Ford 'T', which had motoriz[ed] America and had been an example to all the world, was at last put into retire[ment] after 20 years of honourable service. The changeover to the Model 'A' was made easily and gently, as soon as the Model 'T' had been withdrawn. The Model 'A' which had a pleasing modern line and a four-cylinder 328 cc engi[ne] stayed in production until 1932. It was available in various versions, such as the two or four door sedan, roadster, coupé and the beach wagon. The one shown in the picture is a Victoria Model 'A' (Hubley model, scale 1:20).

86 An American industrialist decided to name his new company after the man he admired most, Abraham Lincoln, President of the United States of America. Thus, in 1909, the Lincoln Motor Company came into being. However, it met with considerable misfortune and was forced into bankruptcy in 1921. It was then taken over by Henry Ford who retained the Lincoln name. In 1928 the eight-cylinder Lincoln was brought out and immediately became famous for its exceptional acceleration and speed. These two qualities often caused it to be used in terrifying battles between t[he] police and liquor smugglers during the years of prohibition (Rio model, scal[e] 1:43).

87 Bentley, one of the most famous companies in the world, began its activities by manufacturing aircraft engines, and was founded by Walter Ow[en] Bentley, an experienced British engineer and racing driver. The first car, designed in 1914, was brought out six years later. It had a three-litre engine [and] was notable for its exceptional strength and large size. It was however, also [a] sports car and before long it gained fame with a series of great sporting successes, and jokingly became referred to as the 'fastest truck in the world'. Between 1920 and 1930 Walter Bentley brought out three competition cars: the three-litre, the $4\frac{1}{2}$-litre and six-litre, and these cars won five races at Le Mans in 1924, 1927, 1928, 1929 and held several world records. A particular[ly] significant victory was achieved at Le Mans in 1929 when Bentleys came in [the] first four places. During the Depression Bentley had to cut down on produc[tion] and it merged with Rolls Royce in 1931. The photograph shows a 1930 Le M[ans] type $4\frac{1}{2}$-litre Bentley (Spot-On model, scale 1:42).

52

Purity of line and amazing mechanical perfection are combined in the
...cedes 'SS' shown in the photograph. It was launched by the Stuttgart
...ory in 1928, after the merger between Daimler and Benz. This sports car
...indeed worthy of the name of Mercedes which was to have even more
...esses in the thirties. The powerful 'SS' was, in fact a descendant of the
...nificent 1923 racing Mercedes and the 'K' with supercharger made in 1927.

It was fitted with a six-cylinder 6800 cc engine and in spite of its great weight,
was capable of a speed of 185 mph, mainly because of the extra power given by
the supercharger. In 1931 the 'SS' was followed by the 'SSK' which had its
cylinder capacity increased to 7100 cc. The photograph shows a 1928 Mercedes
'SS', in a model that captures the unmistakably powerful appearance of this
sports car (Solido model, scale 1:43).

89 In 1929 Isotta Fraschini, who had by now achieved considerable fame both in Italy and abroad, brought out the elegant eight-cylinder car shown in the photograph. However, the company was beginning to feel the effects of the Depression, since the United States was one of their main clients; gradually the production and prestige of Isotta Fraschini began to decline. The excellent model shown in the photograph is of the 1929 '8/A'. Features of note include the lining, the leather upholstery and the folding top. The hood can be opened to reveal the engine, and the steering is operable. (Model made by Carlo Brianza, scale 1:12).

90 This photograph gives a life-size view of the front of the 1929 '8/A' Isotta Fraschini illustrated above. Great skill was needed to reproduce the radiator, lights and the glass over them, the gas-tank cap and the inscriptions 'IF'. (Model made by Carlo Brianza, scale 1:12).

91 When Lancia ceased production of the Lambda in 1931, this car was succeeded by the Dilambda, another high-class vehicle, which had been brought out in 1929. At this time, Lancia had named all its cars after the letters of the Greek alphabet, but later they used other names, such as Artena, Astura, Augusta, Aprilia and Ardea. The Dilambda shown here in the tourer version, had an eight-cylinder 3960 V engine, independent rear suspension and was built on a long or short chassis. About 1,700 were manufactured up until 1937. It had considerable success in America too, where it was known as the Lancia Eight (Rio model, scale 1:43).

92 A magnificent sports car was launched by Fiat in 1929 – the '525 SS'. It was the sports version of the famous '525' of the previous year; the engine still had a cylinder capacity of 3739 cc, but the 'SS' had a supercharger which increased the power from 68 to 88 hp, and the speed from 70 to 75 mph. The average gas consumption was 12 mpg. The photograph shows the slim and elegant '525 SS' sports version. (Model made by Bruno Reggiani for the Fiat Historical Centre, scale 1:5).

93 The 1930 Packard Victoria was one of the company's most successful models, and 48,000 were made in only the first year of production. The eight-cylinder Victoria was a very luxurious car and comparable to the most refined European makes. The photograph shows the convertible version (Lesney model, scale 1:47).

54

91

92

93

94

95

94 The '8c 2300' is one of the most beautiful and famous Alfa Romeos. It came out in 1931, and after a somewhat disappointing start won a great many sporting honours. The photograph shows a spectacular model of the 'Monza' version. Made by a Turin company, this model is about two feet long and is a real connoisseur's piece, worthy of being classed with the prototypes of the most famous model makers. It can be bought already assembled or in an assembly kit and is made up of about 1,500 pieces (Pocher model, scale 1:8).

95 The photograph shows a detail of the engine of the 1931 '8c 2300' Alfa Romeo illustrated above. As well as a complete reproduction of the engine, this model has a trunk which can be opened, a fully operational braking system it can be steered, and the suspension, transmission shaft and engine shaft can operated by means of the crank at the front. The spoked wheels, which are each made up from about 140 pieces, are magnificent (Pocher model, scale 1:

96 Duesenberg: a fabulous name which even today evokes the automobile of one's dreams. These spectacular cars were already in circulation in 1921 and gave great prestige to their owners, but they did not achieve their greatest success until about 1930 when the stupendous Model 'J' was brought out. It h a seven-litre, eight-cylinder engine with an amazing power of 265 hp, capable of reaching a speed of over 115 mph. The photograph shows a 1931 Duesenbe 'J' town coupé (Dugu model, scale 1:43).

96

56

98 99

Even today, the Alfa Romeo '6c 1750' remains a classic among cars and ccupies an important place in the history of Alfa Romeo and of all Italian tomobiles. Its name is due to the six-cylinder 1750 cc engine which was made 1929 and gave its makers considerable commercial and sporting success. e model shown in the photograph, and in the following two, is of a 1932 750' and is part of the Quattroruote Collection. (Model made by Manuel ive Sans, scale 1:12).

This illustration is of the central part of the '6c 1750' Alfa Romeo shown the previous photograph. The modelmaker has made locks for the doors hich are lined with leather, and there is even a little map pocket. The car

is carpeted and has beautifully constructed tires and spoked wheels. (Model made by Manuel Olive Sans, scale 1:12).

99 This photograph shows a view of the driving seat and instrument panel of the remarkable '6c 1750' Alfa Romeo. This is the same model as shown in the previous photographs, and is so realistic that it is almost impossible to distinguish it from the real car. The perfection of line is particularly noticeable, and one of the greatest talents of this model-maker is the enormous precision with which he has reproduced the details. Almost all professionals in this field work from the original detailed drawings which they then reduce in scale. (Model made by Manuel Olive Sans, scale 1:12).

57

100

101

100 In 1911, Louis Chevrolet, a Swiss who had emigrated to America at the beginning of the century, founded his automobile company, backed by William Durant, founder of General Motors. A most skilful technician and driver, Chevrolet involved himself in his work with great enthusiasm and this soon paid dividends. But the racing world still held the main attraction for him, and in 1918 when his company was incorporated into General Motors, he returned to motor racing. The photograph shows a 1932 Chevrolet Roadster (Hubley model, scale 1:20).

101 In 1932, as a result of their vast experience on the racing track, and the experiments with light alloys, Alfa Romeo were able to bring out a racing car of quite revolutionary design which was to gain a great number of victories. This was the 'P.3', which had a 200 hp engine cast in an alloy known as electron, with a cylinder capacity of 2654 cc. Nuvolari drove one of them to victory in the 1932 French Grand Prix, in which 'P.3's' also came second and third. In the same year Caracciola drove a 'P.3' to victory at Monza (Rio model, scale 1:43).

58

One of the most famous names in French motoring history is that of ...ge, which was mentioned so often in the racing chronicles, particularly ...g the twenties. Above all else, Louis Delage would have liked to have ... a racing driver, but unfortunately defective eyesight made this impossible. ...ever, his passion for automobiles was not diminished, and since he could ...drive racing cars he decided to build them. First he worked at Peugeot ...re he acquired his technical experience, and in 1905 he was able to open ...wn workshop where he started by making tourers and later concentrated ...esigning racing cars. His tenacity and enthusiasm were rewarded by success ...only in the pre-war period but also during the twenties when a series of ...iant achievements won him fame. Among his many victories were the

French Grand Prix and the San Sebastian Prize in 1925, a feat which he repeated in 1927 when he also won the European and the British Grand Prix. Famous drivers like the Frenchmen Divo and Benoist also drove Delages to victory. From 1923 to 1925 these racing cars were built with twelve-cylinder 2000 cc V engines, and from 1927 to 1928 with eight-cylinder 1500 cc engines. Even the Delages sold for private use were distinguished by their excellent engines and beautiful lines. Unfortunately, this firm too was adversely affected by the Depression which spread over America and Europe around 1930, and after a period of uncertainty it merged with Delahaye in 1935. The photograph shows one of the beautiful Delages made for private use (Rami model, scale 1:43).

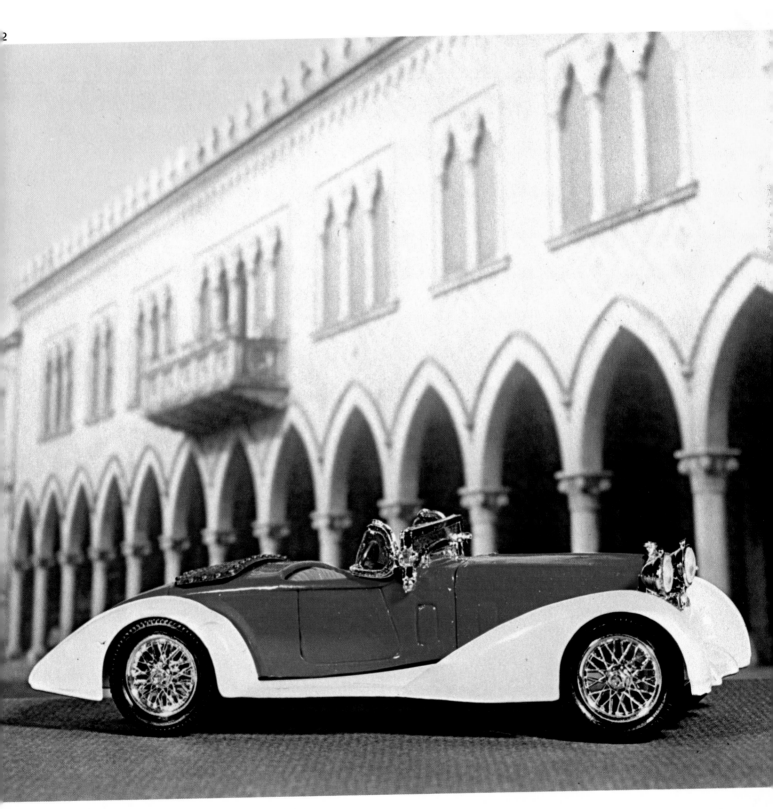

59

103

104

103 In 1932 Sir Henry Royce died, the other partner of the firm, Rolls, having been killed in an air crash much earlier. As a sign of mourning, it is said that the red double R of the Rolls Royce badge was changed to black. The famous Silver Ghost continued for almost twenty years and was followed in 1925 by the Phantom which was made in three successive series. The one illustrated here is a 1932 Henry Sedanca Coupé 'Phantom 11', a magnificent car reproduced here in a superlative model about 56 inches long, which can be bought. It is one of the most beautiful mass-produced models in the world (Pocher model, scale 1:8).

104–105 This illustration shows details of the engine and chassis of the 1932 Phantom 11 Rolls Royce shown in the previous photograph. It is made up of almost 2,000 pieces in plastic, metal, rubber and leather. The doors, hood and trunk can be opened, the steering and lights really work, as do the suspension, braking circuit and windows. The starting handle at the front turns the pistons, connecting rods and crank-shaft (Pocher model, scale 1:8).

60

106

The arrival of the Fiat '508', better known as the 'Balilla', constituted [e]vent of great importance in the motorization of Italy and in the history of great Turin car manufacturer. When presented to the public at the Milan [aut]omobile Show in April of 1932, it immediately became a great success [beca]use of its low cost, low gas consumption and excellent performance. The [car] was to make it the ideal car for the Italian family, and it was launched [by] a huge publicity campaign that turned it into one of the biggest events [of the] time; there was even a popular song about it. The 'Balilla', which was [sold] at 10,800 lire, was a utility car with an extremely well-built four-cylinder [995] cc engine. It had a gas consumption of 30 mpg, a speed of 50 mph and had [plen]ty of space for four people and baggage. The car had an endurance of

185 miles and weighed 1712 lbs. Notable mechanical features included the hydraulic brakes on all four wheels and a complete electric system. Initially, there were three-speed gears, but two years later a four-speed model with a different bodywork was brought out. The photograph shows an excellent reproduction of a 1932 'Balilla 508'. (Model made by Bruno Reggiani for the Fiat Historical Centre, scale 1:5).

107 This photograph shows the front view of the 1932 Fiat 'Balilla 508'. About 64 inches long, it reproduces in every detail the complex structure of the original automobile. (Model made by Bruno Reggiani for the Fiat Historical Centre, scale 1:5).

107

61

108

109

108 After the incomparable Type 41 Royale, Ettore Bugatti turned to the building of a new and aristocratic car to carry on the traditions of this famous French firm. This resulted in the 'Bugatti 50' which was equipped with a 4972 cc engine and was capable of 105 mph. It was judged a true masterpiece of engineering. The most famous coachmakers in France vied with each other to 'dress' this marvellous sports car with a matchless bodywork. The photograph shows a 1932 'Bugatti 50' (Rio model, scale 1:43).

109 In 1933 Fiat presented its '508-S' or 'Balilla Sport'. The coachwork was by Ghia and the power of the engine was increased from 20 to 36 hp giving a speed of 70 mph. Fiat bought the drawings from Ghia and so this attractive sports car was incorporated into Fiat's production programme. Two types were put on sale, the 'Coppa d'Oro' with tapering fenders and the 'Mille Miglia' with helmet fenders. Both competed with enormous success in the big motor races of the day. The photograph shows the Fiat '508-S' (or the 1933 Coppa d'Oro Balilla sports car) in an excellent model made by a Spaniard. (Model made by Manuel Olive Sans for the Fiat Historical Centre, scale 1:5).

110 The amazing precision with which the 1933 508-S Balilla sports car shown above has been modelled, can clearly be seen in this detail showing the steering-wheel, instrument panel, windshield and windshield wipers. (Model made by Manuel Olive Sans for the Fiat Historical Centre, scale 1:5).

110

62

111

112

The unusual body of the 1934 Voisin 22 hp is said to have been inspired ...he work of the famous architect, Le Corbusier. It was certainly one of the ... luxurious automobiles of the time. The founder of the factory, Gabriel ...in, already had a great deal of experience in aircraft construction when, ...e beginning of the twenties, he decided to build his first automobile. ... was the '18 CV' which was immediately a great success. Voisin was a ...ly talented man and when, during the next few years, he built four new ... with 4, 6, 8 and 12 cylinders, they gained enormous admiration, even ...ng his competitors. In the post-war period Voisin set to work on the ...struction of a very small utility car. The photograph shows a 1934 ...in 22 hp (Solido model, scale 1:43).

112 Film stars, millionaires, leaders and influential people in both the United States and abroad vied with each other for the possession of a Duesenberg, the last word in perfection and elegance during the years before and after 1930. Even today, the few surviving Duesenbergs fetch astronomical prices, and unfortunately only a few were made due to the high cost of the materials and the laboriously long hours involved in its construction. Each car was probably built according to the client's instructions. The photograph shows a 1934 Duesenberg 'SJ' which succeeded the famous 'J': it was a gigantic and aristocratic vehicle fitted with a 6880 cc engine plus supercharger and eight cylinders in-line. Like the model above, its shape evokes the 1930s (Rio model, scale 1:43).

63

113

113 1932 is a memorable date in the history of Ford: in that year the V8 engine was introduced and used in the Ford Model B. This eight-cylinder 3622 cc engine with side valves had a 65 hp power and was extremely efficient. Two years later Ford launched a sports car with the same engine considerably increased in power. The photograph shows a 1934 Ford coupé, an automobile that remains in the memory of many motorists of today (A.M.T. model, scale 1:25).

114 Citroën established two successive sensational world records on the Montlhéry track: in 1932 the C6 Rosalie II completed 81,250 miles in 54 days at an average speed of 65 mph, and in 1933 C4 Petite Rosalie completed 187,500 miles in 134 days at an average speed of 55 mph. The Rosalie shown here in the 1934 sedan version was the last old-style vehicle to be made by the famous French company; thus it is a fitting close to an era in the history of the automobile (Norev model, scale 1:43).

114